KIDS and DOGS

A Professional's Guide to Helping Families

Colleen Pelar, CPDT, CDBC

DREAM**DOG**

PRODUCTIONS

Kids and Dogs
A Professional's Guide to Helping Families
Colleen Pelar, CPDT
Published by:
C&R Publishing, a division of
Dream Dog Productions, LLC
PO Box 4227
Woodbridge VA 22194-4227

www.dreamdogproductions.com

Copyright 2009, Colleen Pelar

Pelar, Colleen
Kids and Dogs
P.cm.
Includes index
ISBN 978-1-933562-06-3
1. Pets 2. Dogs

Cover by www.nutscreative.com

Printed in China

All photos courtesy of Shutterstock.com with the following exceptions: Vicki Gotcher, p. 18, 45 (first in left column, third in center column, bottom in right column); Pam Nashman, pp. 22, 23, 24, 37, 109; Martha Walker, p. 33; Colleen Pelar, pp. 35, 56, 71 (bottom), 84, 86, 98, 107, 110, 112; Keely Bovais, p. 45 (bottom in first column); Dogs & Storks, p. 50; Kevin Lamarque, p. 92; Robin Bennett, p. 105; Maureen Daniels, p. 96, 101

10   9   8   7   6   5   4   3   2

Contents

● ● ● ● ● ● ● ● ● ● ● ● ● ● ●

Kids & Dogs: A Professional's Guide to Helping Families

Acknowledgements

● ● ● ● ● ● ● ● ● ● ● ● ● ● ● ● ●

I'm an introvert by nature. When I taught my first dog-training class in September of 1991, I was terrified. With a quiet, quivering voice, I worked to teach people how to train their dogs, but was convinced that at any moment they would all come to learn I was a fraud. Only one thing kept me going: my incredible love of dogs.

So bit by bit over the years, I learned to develop what my friends and family call my "dog-training persona," an outgoing alternate ego who isn't afraid to get up in front of a group and look a little foolish—as long as I'm talking about dogs. And, with time, I have become more and more comfortable with my dog-training persona, which has allowed me to speak in front of groups much larger than a dog class. I've been honored to speak at the Association of Pet Dog Trainers, Professional Animal Behavior Associates, Canadian Association of Professional Pet Dog Trainers, and National Pet Sitters Association conferences, and, much to my surprise, I love it!

But, you know, that fraud alert still plagues me at times. As a result, I've dedicated myself to learning as much about dogs as I can. The more I learn, the more questions I have. Fortunately, I am blessed to have a wonderful family and group of friends who encourage me to continue that learning process and to be brave when it's time to share that learning with others although my natural inclination is to hide in the background. And I'm so grateful to them because, by stepping out of my comfort zone, I have learned so much more about dogs—and myself—than I ever dreamed. So thanks are in order.

First off, I must thank my husband, Jack, who is not a dog lover, but loves me enough to live with dogs simply because they mean so much to me. (How did we wind up together, you ask? I sure don't know, but I'm so glad we did.) Thanks also to my sons, Justin, Kyle, and Brandon, who fill my life with love, laughter, and quite a bit of chaos. I'm so blessed to have the four of you.

My fantastic business partner, Robin Bennett, inspires (and occasionally exasperates) me with her incredible productivity and constant flow of great ideas. I'm always racing just to keep up. Robin and Pam Nashman (a wonderful friend and dog trainer) were the driving force behind this book, which is based on a presentation I first gave at the 2008 APDT conference. Within 5 minutes of my getting off the stage, they told me that I needed to turn it into a book. And Pam made sure that happened. She is the nicest "bulldozer" I could ever hope for, and she helped in more ways than I could ever list.

I am also blessed to work with the incredible staff at All About Dogs (Keely Bovais, Diana Craig, Eileen Fulk, Vicki Gotcher, Chris Johnson, Vicky Shields, and Martha Walker) and to laugh and recharge monthly with the Lunch Bunch (Penelope Brown, Susan McCullough, Pat Miller, Victoria Schade, and Pam Wanveer). Thanks to all of you for being a part of my life and for loving dogs as much as I do.

Leslie Brier, Frances Dauster, Debra Ekman, Shirley and Bob Hendel, Helen Hershner, Candice McKing, Jill Siegel, Julie Szabo, and Natalie York all made suggestions that improved the final product. Thank you!

This book is for dog aficionados, the dog nuts of the world (you know who you are). Thank you for all the work you do to help dogs every day. It matters.

Let's Get Started!

● ● ● ● ● ● ● ● ● ● ● ● ● ● ● ● ●

Parents who want to raise their children with a dog have a really tough job, one without much support or even acknowledgement. There are few sources that teach a parent how to supervise kids and dogs. The assumption is that every conscientious parent will do a good job.

We have a cultural perception that dog behavior is common knowledge—everyone knows about dogs—yet dog aficionados spend lifetimes learning about it. Living with kids and dogs is far more complex than people are led to believe.

Dog aficionados can play a vitally important role in making sure that kid and dog interactions are not only safe, but also a positive part of a child's development and a secure, happy, enriching relationship for both the dog and the child. In fact, I believe we are obligated to do everything we can to help dogs by helping the general public better understand the animals we love.

Are You a Dog Aficionado?

Dog aficionados are dog trainers, dog behavior consultants, veterinarians, vet clinic staff, shelter workers, rescue volunteers, groomers, dog walkers, animal control officers, dog daycare staff, boarding facility employees, breeders, holistic health care providers, pet-supply store owners, pet sitters, therapy-dog handlers, puppy raisers, writers who specialize in dog topics, and many more. In short, anyone who works with dogs other than his or her own is a dog aficionado.

Dog-training books say, "Control your kids," and they expect parents control them to a level that seems pretty unrealistic to anyone who has ever been around a two year old for more than 20 minutes. Parents are exhorted to make sure their kids don't run, don't scream, don't make loud noises, avoid abrupt movements, and never look a dog in the face. Who could ensure that none of those things happen all day, everyday, for the next twelve or more years? That's not very realistic advice when you're actually in the same household with children and dogs.

Behavior isn't Black and White

Behavior is rarely all good or all bad. Think of it as a continuum, ranging from one extreme to the other, but with plenty of time in the middle. Parents can easily see how this relates to their children's behavior (and their own), but often need to have it pointed out for them to realize that it is true of their dog's behavior as well. I've used a red, yellow, and green color scheme throughout the book to illustrate the range of behavior from worrisome to wonderful.

Parenting books, on the other hand, imply that dogs are dangerous, unpredictable, and scary. These books contain more fear-mongering than actual guidance for parents. Although many contain instructions on how to treat a dog bite, few give any advice for avoiding one. Ultimately, the basic advice that most parents get is

➤ Never leave a dog and child alone.
➤ Supervise everything.

That's perfectly good advice, but it doesn't go far enough! Life is filled with good moments and bad moments. No one teaches parents what supervision means, what to look for, what's important, what's not important, and when to intervene. And since parents don't know any of that information, they repeatedly miss signs of impending trouble. Then, when a child is bitten, dog aficionados' e-mail lists go crazy. "What are those parents doing? Oh, my goodness, what were they thinking? How could they have let that happen?"

Well, they didn't know. And the reason they didn't know is because we didn't teach them. Let's fix that.

Scenes from Real Life

Until you have lived with kids and dogs, it can be hard to imagine what it is like. When everyone is active, it's really challenging to supervise every single interaction because kids and dogs move from room to room and from activity to activity.

Sometimes a dog aficionado who is not a parent will share a story with me that seems extreme to him or her and just sounds like a regular day to me—because I have been in a similar situation with my own kids and dogs.

This father is trying to set up a nice interaction between the baby and the dog, but he doesn't see that the dog is uncomfortable.

Here are just a few scenarios that I've encountered while working with kids and dogs. Some of these resulted in dog bites; others did not. I decided not to list which category each interaction fell into because the temperament of the dog and the child, the quality of their relationship, and the level of management and supervision that the parents provide greatly affect how a situation will turn out.

- Two-month-old baby in bouncy seat on the floor with dog lying beside. Mom walks across the room to get a book.
- Four-month-old baby lying on a blanket and kicking a toy that hangs above her. Baby laughs as the toy's bells jangle. Dog comes over to investigate.
- Seven-month-old baby crawls toward dog napping in the corner.
- One-year-old child, who can stand by hanging onto furniture, falls down on his bottom near the dog.
- Eighteen-month-old toddler sits down in the hallway every time the dog approaches because the dog has knocked her over many times when rushing past.
- Two-year-old toddler runs ahead of his father into the living room and steps on the dog's tail as he climbs on the couch.
- Two-year-old toddler drops a napkin on the floor when trying to put it in the garbage can. She and the dog reach for it at the same time.
- Three-year-old child doesn't want to take a nap. He throws a tantrum and flings a wooden puzzle board, which hits the dog.
- Three-year-old child wants the dog to wear her blanket as a cape. It slips off, but the girl repeatedly grabs the dog and wraps the blanket around him.
- Four-year-old child gets a flashlight and shines it repeatedly at the dog to "make his eyes light up."
- Four-year-old child sits on the coffee table and pets the dog with her feet.
- Five-year-old child plays in an empty box. He stands up inside it and walks "like a robot" around the room.
- Five-year-old child plays "dentist" with the dog. She brushes the dog's teeth (with her own toothbrush) and even gives the dog a sticker for a good checkup.
- Six-year-old child watches a video lying on the floor using the dog as a pillow.
- Six-year-old child builds a fort out of couch cushions. The dog comes in to investigate. The fort collapses on them both.

- Seven-year-old child puts the dog's bowl down and then decides to move it. As the dog is eating, the child reaches down and picks up the bowl.
- Seven-year-old child is having a bad day. She starts crying and goes to her room. The dog follows her in. She cuddles with the dog while she cries and won't let him get off the bed when he's ready to leave.
- Eight-year-old child crashes his bike near where the dog is tethered.
- Eight-year-old child likes sliding down the stairs on her bottom, which entails lots of shouting and laughing. The dog watches warily from the bottom.
- Nine-year-old child drops his cereal bowl. Cereal, milk, and broken pottery are scattered across the kitchen floor. He pushes the dog out of the room.
- Nine-year-old child is creating a Styrofoam solar system. A ball rolls off the kitchen table. The dog grabs the ball, takes it to his crate, and hovers over it.

Playmate or Nanny?

It often seems that dogs are expected to be a child's favorite playmate, perpetually available and eager to play. At the same time, however, we also ask the dog to act like a nanny by self-handicapping so the child always wins.

We don't expect a child's sibling will accept every invitation to play, lose every contest, and carefully control his impulses so as never to overwhelm the child. Let's be realistic about what we ask of dogs.

- Ten-year-old child is playing a computer game. When he wins, he spins around in the chair, cheering and swinging his feet. He accidentally kicks the dog.
- Ten-year-old child opens the door to let a friend enter. The dog darts out. Both girls chase the dog through the neighborhood.
- Eleven-year-old child accidentally slams the car door on the dog's tail.
- Eleven-year-old child is annoyed about being told to let the dog out, so she grabs his collar and drags him to the door.

- Twelve-year-old middle-schooler finds an old t-shirt in a drawer and dresses the dog in it.
- Twelve-year-old middle-schooler plays tug with the dog. Between rounds, she holds the toy above her head. The dog jumps for it.
- Thirteen-year-old teenager carries a stack of books up the stairs to his room. He trips and the books slide and fall down the stairs toward the dog.
- Fourteen-year-old teenager goes sledding. Dog chases her down the hill and nips at her coat.

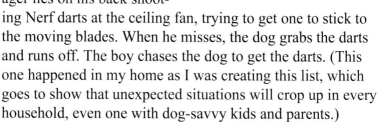

- Fifteen-year-old teenager dumps a basket of laundry on the dog's head.
- Sixteen-year-old teenager gets annoyed by the dog's barking and throws a shoe to distract the dog.
- Seventeen-year-old teenager lies on his back shooting Nerf darts at the ceiling fan, trying to get one to stick to the moving blades. When he misses, the dog grabs the darts and runs off. The boy chases the dog to get the darts. (This one happened in my home as I was creating this list, which goes to show that unexpected situations will crop up in every household, even one with dog-savvy kids and parents.)

Notice that in most of these incidents, there's only one child, one dog, and a parent nearby. The dog is not being overtly aggressive and the child is not being deliberately unkind. Still it would be tough to be the adult in charge of keeping everything calm and relaxed. Supervising kids and dogs is hard. It gets harder with each additional kid and/or dog, but the reality is, even with only one child and one dog, it's never easy.

Good kids and good dogs will have miscommunications every day.

According to the Centers for Disease Control, nearly 2.8 million children are bitten by a dog each year. In most cases, the child knows the dog well. It's usually the family dog or a dog belonging to a close friend, relative, or neighbor. Leash laws and dangerous-dog ordinances won't prevent many dog bites to children because most occur in a household setting and are the result of a miscommunication.

Not All Bites Are Created Equal

Janis Bradley's book, *Dogs Bite . . . But Balloons and Slippers are More Dangerous*, has very interesting statistics on dog bites and other injuries:

- Most dog-bite injuries are minor punctures and lacerations that require no professional treatment.
- Of all dog bites treated in the emergency room, only 1.6% need to be admitted to the hospital for further treatment. The rest are treated and released the same day.
- Emergency rooms treat over 13 times more sports-related injuries than dog bites.
- 92.4% of dog bites cause no injury and an additional 7.5% are considered "fast healing, with no lasting impairment." That equals 99.9% of dog bites!

When you get a call about a dog biting a child, be sure to ask many questions. Bites vary widely in intensity—and in perception. You'll hear scary bites described as nips and puppy mouthing called an attack. Only by using follow-up questions will you get enough detail to learn what actually happened. Ask questions about who was in the room, where each individual was positioned before the bite, what activities were occurring, whether the owner saw any early-warning signs, and what kind of damage (if any) resulted from the bite.

In my opinion, any bite to a child is an emergency. The family needs to get a qualified dog professional's feedback about how serious the incident was and what changes will need to be made to prevent another bite from occurring.

Kids & Dogs: A Professional's Guide to Helping Families

I passionately believe that we can radically reduce the number of dog bites to children if we tackle the problem head on. The way I see it, we have to implement a four-pronged approach of teaching dog owners, parents, kids, and dogs what each of them needs to know to interact happily with each other.

Dog aficionados could teach parents what they need to know—parents are eager to learn—but to do that, we need to have a better understanding of how kids and dogs actually behave so we can meet parents in the middle. Most parents are doing their best. However, on the kid-and-dog front, parents aren't doing as well as they could be because they don't know everything they need to know.

Western society generally has the view that we all know dogs because we've all had dogs; therefore everybody knows everything they need to know about dogs. Unfortunately, that's a gross oversimplification. It's simply not true. Parents have very good intentions, but they don't realize how much they don't know about dogs. Books, movies, and TV have given the impression that dogs are simple to understand. Many owners would be stunned to hear that trainers go to conferences and seminars, spending days at a time talking about dogs and that we still have lots of questions!

With education, parents can prevent dog bites

The advice we give parents must be realistic, and it has to be as easy to understand and follow as you can possibly make it. Sometimes, trainers create extraordinary behavior modification plans and proudly present them to the client, only to hear the client say, "I can't do this. It's too hard." The kid-and-dog issue is similar. Parents have a lot on their plates. They need to feel that we are making their lives easier, not harder. The easier our ideas are to implement, the more likely

"All My Kids Have Four Legs"

I've seen this quote on t-shirts and baseball caps at lots of dog-related events. While nearly 83 percent of American adults have a child by the age of 35, many dog aficionados choose not to have children. I can't find actual statistics, but the proportion of dog aficionados who do not have kids is definitely higher than the national average of 17%.

At All About Dogs, our training facility, we currently have 10 trainers, only 4 of whom have children. I think that percentage is about average. When a dog aficionado who doesn't have kids works with families, two challenges can arise that complicate helping parents with kid-and-dog interactions.

First, dog aficionados do far more management than they realize. I often hear that a dog having trouble in a new home did well with an experienced foster owner. The foster owner was familiar with dog behavior, intervened early and often, body-blocked effortlessly, handled the leash with ease, and made sure to meet the dog's physical and mental needs—all without giving it much thought.

For new dog owners (or owners who have "more dog" than they expected), it can be very helpful to learn, in detail, all the things dog aficionados do without thinking. 'Don't think you do anything special? Ask a friend to do a dog-related task in your home. For example, if you ask someone unfamiliar with your dog's quirks to put the dog's leash on and take him out for a potty break, will that person do it in such a way that minimizes jumping and overexcitement? Will he or she be able to get out the door with a single dog when others crowd around? Pay attention to the things you want to say to your friend to make the task simpler. These are the kinds of suggestions you should be making to dog owners. Share your ideas. They're valuable.

The second challenge is that people who don't live with kids sometimes don't realize how hard it is to supervise children. Asking a parent to ensure that a toddler never runs or screams near a dog is like asking a dog owner to be sure their puppy never barks or jumps. Sooner or later, it's gonna happen. We need to make sure our advice takes this into account. Kids are impulsive, inconsistent, and fast—just like dogs.

If we focus on first making sure families adopt the right dog for their household and then giving the families tips that encourage safe interactions with lots of fun together and adequate time apart, many kid-and-dog issues will be avoided altogether.

parents are to follow through. This factor alone makes a huge difference.

In most dog-bite incidents, there was an adult close by. Our case files are full of such stories. Before the bite, few of these parents had any worries about their dog, but when I ask questions, it's clear that there were warning signs that the parents missed.

Seventy-seven percent of dog bites to children are on the face. That's a big deal. Almost all those bites could be prevented if parents know how to interpret what they are seeing. Dog aficionados have an obligation to prevent as many injuries as we can.

Dr. Ian Dunbar's Bite Level Assessment

LEVEL 1: Obnoxious or aggressive behavior, but no skin contact by teeth.

LEVEL 2: Skin contact by teeth, but no skin punctures. However, there may be nicks (less than 1/10" deep) and slight bleeding caused by forward or lateral movement of teeth against skin, but no vertical punctures.

LEVEL 3: One to four punctures from a single bite with no puncture deeper than half the length of the dog's canine teeth. May be lacerations in a single direction, caused by victim pulling hand away, owner pulling dog away, or gravity (e.g., little dog jumps, bites, and drops to floor).

LEVEL 4: One to four punctures from a single bite with at least one puncture deeper than half the length of the dog's canine teeth. May also have deep bruising around the wound (dog held on for x seconds and bore down) or lacerations in both directions (dog held on and shook its head from side to side).

LEVEL 5: Multiple-bite incident with at least two Level 4 bites.

LEVEL 6: Flesh consumed or victim dead.

To prevent dog bites to children, we need to focus on the relationship between kids and dogs. I know of a 4-year-old boy who, when he was at his father's house, was allowed to ride a Great Dane mix regularly. Great Danes are not horses! Dog aficionados don't encourage children to ride dogs, but when a dog is tolerant, parents will often think there's no harm in the child having some fun.

Don't you think that by allowing the boy to ride the dog whenever he chose, the relationship between the boy and the dog was damaged? (Not to mention the relationship between the dog and the adult. How frustrating it must be for a dog to try to communicate with a person who isn't seeing your stress signals.) One day, the dog bit the boy on the forehead. Suddenly, without warning? Only to a parent who hadn't been taught what to look for and when to intervene.

I also have photos of children killed by dogs. Parents kill many more children than dogs do, but infanticide winds up being a local news story. Dog-related deaths often make national news. They're horrific, no doubt about it. Statistically speaking, the risk is low; however one child being killed is too many. We should be able to avoid that. There isn't any reason why we can't dramatically reduce the number of injuries caused by dogs, if we, as dog aficionados, help people "get it," help them to understand there's much more to dogs than they realize.

There's a big discrepancy between what dog aficionados recommend people do with dogs and what just happens naturally. I once spent a few minutes watching a tiny Chihuahua wearing a tutu at a small community fair. It will surprise no one to learn that three 8-year-old girls were drawn to the Chihuahua, asked for permission, and then began petting her.

The Chihuahua's owner paid no attention to the girls at all. She had turned away to talk to an adult, while these girls (who had never met this dog before) crowded around her, picked her up, and petted her on top of her head. By little girl standards, those girls were being lovely to that dog. They had good intentions, they were gentle, and they were very interested in the little dog.

But by dog standards, it was a terrible interaction. We would never recommend strangers rush up to a dog, surround it, pick it up, and have three people simultaneously pet the dog. You may imagine what this little dog's facial expression looked like as this occurred. Her mouth was tightly closed, and she was staring intently at her oblivious owner.

This Chihuahua is licking her lips.

The dog's owner didn't help at all. Why should she? She knew she had a good dog, and since good dogs would never bite, there was really no need to get involved. Besides, as far as she could tell, her dog was content. The dog wasn't flailing or barking. Instead, she became still and tolerated the interaction. From the owner's point of view, the dog loved the attention. If not, why would she dress her dog in a tiny pink tutu and take her to a fair?

For dog aficionados, the desire to throttle this owner is strong. On the other hand, I think this owner is doing the best she can with insufficient information. She hasn't been taught how to read her dog's body language. All she knows is that children should ask permission before petting a dog—and they did—but no one has taught this owner how to set her dog up for success or to be a good advocate for the dog she clearly loves.

The Worst Thing You Can Do

I do not think rehoming a dog is the worst thing you can do. I don't even think euthanizing an aggressive dog is the worst thing you can do. In fact, I'll argue that in some cases these can be acts of kindness. As dog aficionados, we want people to commit to living with and loving their dogs for a lifetime, and many of our careers focus on making just that happen. But sometimes circumstances can change.

Adding children to a household can make things very different for a dog. Most dogs adjust very well, but for some, it's incredibly stressful. It's tempting to think that the dog only needs time and things will get easier for everybody. In some cases, this is true. But if, after everyone has had time to get to know one another and the parents have made adjustments to their household, the dog is still unhappy, then it's time to consider what is best for everyone, including the dog.

I have had many clients tell me that rehoming their dog is not an option under any circumstances. While I admire their commitment, I sometimes wonder if they are looking at things from the dog's point of view. Is it best for the dog to live the rest of his life in an environment that makes him feel stressed? Is it fair to expect a skittish dog to tune out rambunctious children at play? Is it safe to keep a dog with serious resource-guarding issues in a household that includes so many things he'd like to guard from children who can't read his signals? Is it relevant that the dog won't come inside if the children are around? Is this what you want for your dog?

Dogs live in the moment. When my kids were little, I dreamed about my youngest going to preschool. The thought of having two and a half hours alone twice a week sounded so appealing to me. Knowing that each stage is temporary—and having an idea of what was ahead—helped me get through stressful days. But keep in mind that there were more than seven years from the time my first child was born until the last one was old enough for preschool. If a dog is unhappy or stressed in the household, is it fair to say that things will get easier in two, three, four, or more years? I really think that kind of life sentence is the worst thing we can do to dogs who are unhappy in their current living situation.

Dog aficionados joke that families should rehome their children rather than their dogs. Since that isn't going to happen, our responsibility is to help people understand that sometimes the kindest thing to do is to make a difficult decision about what is in the best interest of the dog they love.

That event showed that this little Chihuahua is likely going to be let down by the person she trusts more than anyone in the world, every day, for the rest of her life. Over and over, she'll find herself in uncomfortable situations where she cannot rely on her owner to help her. If one day she bites a little girl who picks her up for a quick cuddle, the community at large will call it an unprovoked bite . . . because we all know that good dogs don't bite.

So, how can dog aficionados help? Every day each of us interacts with people and their dogs. If we work together, we can make an extraordinary difference in the lives of dogs—all dogs, not just the ones we work with directly.

There are six basic things dogs wish people knew:

- ➤ The "Good-Dog Myth" Hurts All Dogs
- ➤ There's No "One Size Fits All" Solution
- ➤ The Difference Between Tolerance and Enjoyment
- ➤ Good Intentions Aren't Enough
- ➤ What to Look for and When to Intervene
- ➤ Teens Can be as Tough as Toddlers

If we could just impart these principles to parents, most kid-and-dog problems would go away. So, let's get started!

Kids & Dogs: A Professional's Guide to Helping Families

The First Thing Dogs Wish People Knew is . . .
The "Good-Dog Myth" Hurts All Dogs

● ● ● ● ● ● ● ● ● ● ● ● ● ● ● ● ● ● ●

Our definition of what it means to be a good dog has gotten far more rigid over the years. Today, we've got this idea that good dogs don't bite—under any circumstances. A good dog enjoys people all the time. A good dog is equally comfortable with family and strangers. A good dog loves kids. A good dog never needs downtime. A good dog will stand still and allow anyone to probe through his fur in search of a tick.

The Stakes Are Higher

As our neighborhoods change, our attitudes about dogs change too. When I was a child, kids were told to avoid certain dogs because they might bite. Occasionally, a dog would bite a child, and often the child would be lectured. "Didn't I tell you to leave that dog alone?"

Now the most likely result would be a call to animal control even if the bite was very minor (as most dog bites are). Neighbors don't know each other as well as they used to. Because of this, a parent is less likely to walk up the street and talk about an incident in which a dog threatened a child.

These days it's common to hear of lawsuits and homeowners' insurance cancellations. There are many more rules and regulations regarding our dogs, but so far, we aren't any safer because we haven't addressed the true issues. We must focus on

- Showing dog owners how to set their dogs up for success
- Teaching parents what to look for and when to intervene
- Coaching children how to be good friends to dogs
- Socializing dogs so they'll be comfortable around people

How many of us have a dog who meets that description? It's not only unrealistic; it's unfair!

We expect more from dogs than we do from people. Is it fair to say that a good person would never shout? Or become impatient with someone else? Or have a bad day and take it out on others? Or be uncomfortable when an acquaintance or stranger touched them? Of course not! We recognize that human behavior is complex and prone to peaks and valleys. A person can have a bad moment—many of them in fact—and still be considered a good person overall.

You may argue that people are in a different category. Instead, let's compare dogs to another household pet: cats. It's quite common for someone to have a cat that does not like strangers, only allows certain kinds of physical interactions, and behaves aggressively if a person makes the cat uncomfortable.

Cooter, a cat with attitude

No one is surprised by this or expects anything different. There are an untold number of cats that fit this description, and still their owners rightly argue that they are good cats. Yet a dog with similar concerns is somehow not a "good dog."

We ask dogs to give us a lifetime of tolerance, and for the most part, they do! It's important, though, to be aware of what we are asking. We need to recognize that there are different boundaries of acceptable behavior for household adults, household children, and people who don't live with the dog, be they friends or strangers.

When children are very young, parents think nothing of picking them up whenever the mood strikes. We manipulate their bodies to get them dressed and hold them still to bathe them and wash their faces. But by the time a child is 2, he's usually establishing some boundaries, and when the child is 4, "I can do it myself" is a common refrain.

How do parents respond? We applaud their development and respect their autonomy. Start looking at kids' shoes when you are in the grocery store. There are many children wearing shoes on the wrong feet or opting for the ease of pull-on boots because it's important to them to have some control over their bodies and their environment.

Of course, dogs are not children. Dog owners touch their dogs many times a day, and some of those interactions will not change over the course of a lifetime. I've never seen a dog put the leash on by herself or brush her own coat, for example. Dogs do need to allow their families to handle their bodies regularly.

Yet most people seem to believe that good dogs allow strangers the same liberties that they grant to trusted family members. How did this belief evolve? How often does a stranger need to touch an unfamiliar dog? The answer is: rarely. Veterinarians will need to be

able to examine the dog, but there's really no need for your next-door neighbor to be able to scratch your dog's haunches just because he feels like doing so.

Choose a vet who is gentle and patient

The whole "good dog" concept makes me cranky. We have unrealistic expectations and standards as to how a "good dog" behaves. Consequently, we are not giving dogs the support they need and deserve.

As dog aficionados, one of our primary responsibilities is to help people better understand dogs. The challenge is to do it in such a way that we don't seem to be preaching. Dog owners believe they know a lot about dogs—and they do—but when filtered through the good-dog lens, that information becomes distorted. Our job is help people see dogs more objectively and to be clear that recognizing the good and the bad doesn't mean they'll love dogs any less. Instead, removing the rose-colored glasses will allow them to be better advocates for their dogs and will actually improve the relationship between them.

Many of our clients believe that dog trainers' dogs are perfect. I used to think so too. In fact, when I started training, I was embarrassed to tell people that I was a trainer because my dogs weren't perfect. The more trainers' dogs I met, the more I realized that dog aficionados love dogs as they are and are generally pretty accepting of normal dog behavior, even when it doesn't match the societal standard of a good dog. It was such a relief to me to see that I didn't need perfect robot dogs to be a good trainer!

Sharing stories with clients can give them similar relief. My favorite class to teach is Relaxing Rowdy Rovers, which is specifically designed for dog-aggressive dogs. Often people will tell me that they are afraid their dog is too bad for the class. Too bad for training? That's what we do! (On rare occasions, I meet a dog who cannot be safely managed in our highly structured environment, and then I'll recommend private lessons. But most dogs do very well in Relaxing Rowdy Rovers.)

Dundee inspired me to become a dog trainer

I'm especially committed to these students because I myself once had a reactive dog, and I had difficulty finding a trainer who would work with us. I was extremely aware that others considered Dundee a "bad dog," and that really hurt me because I adored her and wanted everyone to see all her wonderful qualities.

Letting your students know that you've lived with and loved less-than-perfect dogs can build common ground. At All About Dogs, we are fortunate to have a large staff. We have lots of stories to share about shy dogs, dogs with separation anxiety, dogs who become easily aroused, dogs who demand attention, dogs who are uncomfortable with strangers, and dogs who steal socks, just to list a few. These are dog trainers' dogs, and we love them whole-heartedly.

Once your clients know that you are not judging their dogs, they'll be more open to hearing what you say. Look for and acknowledge good qualities. Tell the students why you are making specific suggestions. Say "It looks like Koda is uncomfortable with Pixie so close. Let's try moving Koda a little farther away to see if that helps her to focus better." When Koda suddenly regains her ability to focus, the owner will become aware of how much space Koda needs to feel less stressed around other dogs. If you hadn't mentioned that her proximity to Pixie was bothering Koda, the owners might think you were moving her for an entirely different reason and thus would be less likely to notice Koda's concerns and possibly increase Koda's unease in the future.

The dog in front is stressed and trying to get away

Meeting a Dog

It's vital to teach kids how to interact with unfamiliar dogs. Childish excitement could be interpreted as a threat by inexperienced dogs.

When dog aficionados take the time to explain the three steps for meeting a dog and allow children to practice these skills with social, appropriate dogs under supervision, the benefits are far-reaching. Kids are going to approach unfamiliar dogs whether we teach them how to do it or not, but a few minutes of your time can have long-lasting effects for the dogs these children will meet in the future.

Step 1 - Ask the Owner

Teach kids not to rush toward a dog. Encourage them to stop about 5 feet away and ask the owner, "May I pet your dog?" Sometimes the answer will be no. Many dogs don't live with kids and are not comfortable with them. So if the dog's owner says no, that's okay. Remind kids that there are lots of other dogs who would love to be petted by them.

If the owner says yes, then the children must ask the dog.

Step 1 - Ask the Owner

Step 2 - Ask the Dog

Do Not Skip This Step! Tell kids that dogs don't use words but instead rely on body language. Pantomime emotions such as anger, fear, and excitement to show the kids that they use body language too.

Have the children make a fist with the palm pointed down. Then they can slowly extend their arm for the dog to sniff their hand. Teaching the kids to curl their fingers in minimizes the risk of a dog nipping their fingers.

When the dog is being given the opportunity to sniff, watch his body language.

- Does he come forward with loose, waggy motions? That's definitely a yes.

- Does he lean forward for a quick sniff and seem comfortable? Also a yes.

- Does he turn his face away from your child's hand? Back away? Bark? Move behind the owner? Look anxious and unsettled? Growl? These are all no's.

Unfortunately some owners don't understand or respect their dog's decision and will drag the dog forward saying, "Oh, he's fine. He loves kids. You can pet him." DON'T! Do not ever allow children to pet a dog that does not approach them willingly.

Step 2 - Ask the Dog

Step 3 - Pet the Dog

If the owner said yes and the dog said yes, the kids can pet the dog. Tell the kids that they need to be careful of a dog's sensitive eyes and ears. Most dogs don't like to be petted on top of their heads, but nearly all people pet dogs this way—it's a hardwired human behavior. There is a blind spot on top of a dog's head. If he sees a child's hand moving toward that area, the natural inclination is for him to tilt his head up and watch where the hand is going. Now the child's hand is reaching right over the dog's teeth—not a very good place for that hand to be.

Suggest that the children stroke the side of the dog's neck, rub under his chin, scratch his chest, or pet along his back. Most dogs prefer slow, gentle strokes to rapid pat-pat-patting.

Step 3 - Pet the Dog

The Second Thing Dogs Wish People Knew is . . .
There's No "One Size Fits All" Solution
● ● ● ● ● ● ● ● ● ● ● ● ● ● ● ● ● ● ●

Parents are often told that there are a few simple steps they need to follow to make sure their dog is safe with children, but this is too simplistic and misleading. For example, parents are told to make the child "alpha" over the dog by, among other things, holding the child above the dog, never to allow the dog to eat before the child, and to encourage the child to give cues. These techniques are often written about in conjunction with old-fashioned training methods and are supplemented by the advice that the parents should handle the dog's body often to prepare the dog for living with children.

Most dog aficionados have moved away from the "alpha" paradigm, but unfortunately, if you do a quick Google search, you'll see those methodologies are still publicly promoted. Parents are going to get a considerable amount of conflicting information from the Internet. Our job is to supplement and reframe what they've found to make it useful, applicable, and above all, correct.

The idea that an adult dog would find a young child "dominant" is laughable to me. I've read that wearing an infant in a front carry pack will help a dog respect the child. Really? Even when the baby is later lying on the floor kicking his feet and cooing? Somehow the dog is supposed to see the infant as a leader? I don't think so.

This isn't to say that I don't believe dogs should ever listen to kids. It's wonderful and inspiring to have kids participate in dog care and, in doing so, they'll give the dog various cues. The difference is that the dog is listening because a parent is there gently supporting—and if necessary, reinforcing—the cues. By 2 years old, my children would cue many behaviors. They'd tell the dog to stay, then carry the food bowl, set it down, and exuberantly release the dog from the stay. It was great fun for everyone. But I was always right there, making sure everything worked according to plan.

Who is in charge? Neither. Both need an adult to care for them.

On the flip side, my boys would sometimes encourage dogs to do something that wasn't allowed, such as approaching the table during a meal or jumping for a toy. They gave conflicting cues, spoke over one another, jostled for position, changed their minds midsentence, and generally acted like kids. It can be very confusing for a dog living with youngsters.

Sometimes, I expected the dog to listen to the kids; other times, I didn't. I never actually sat down and clearly defined my expectations (though life would have been much easier for the dog if I had), but in the end, I developed a pattern that we follow to this day. If one of my sons is standing still, within 2 feet of the dog (but not touching him), and is giving a cue (but not repeating it over and over), then I expect the dog to listen. I will help my child if needed to ensure the interaction goes well, avoiding frustration on the part of the child or the dog.

On the other hand, if my son is chasing one of his brothers around the house and shouts "sit" as he flies by, the dog can ignore that request. Or if one of the boys is lying under the coffee table and calling "come, come, come," the dogs are under no obligation to obey. The dogs only have to comply when the kids are calm, clear, and consistent. Or, in other words, when the kids are acting like leaders (not "Alpha!"). Dogs typically respond better to children as the kids mature, which is as it should be.

Context is hugely important to dogs. What is going on, who is involved, where you are, all of these things play a role in how a dog behaves. In my view, family dogs are the parents' responsibility. The parent, not the child, is responsible for ensuring that the dog behaves as desired.

Many people advocate training a dog to accept rough handling in preparation for living with a child. That sounds good in theory. Certainly, it's a plus if your dog can tolerate being touched all over. So teaching the dog to accept, even enjoy, handling is beneficial. I'll even go so far as to say that you should do some handling that is rougher than normal (but never hurtful).

I'm not convinced, however, that this in any way increases your child's safety around your dog. Just because your dog allows you, a trusted adult, to be rough with him is no guarantee that he will allow anyone else—especially a child—to manhandle him. Canine learning is context specific. Most dogs tolerate more from familiar people than strangers. They will put up with even more from people they love and trust, but often a dog doesn't feel the same level of trust with a child that he feels with an adult because the child's

My Rule for When a Dog Should Listen to a Child

If one of my sons is standing still, within 2 feet of the dog (but not touching him), and is giving a cue (but not repeating it over and over), then I expect the dog to listen. I will help my child if needed to ensure the interaction goes well, avoiding frustration on the part of the child or the dog.

Crawling—The First Surprise

It's rare for me to get a call about a kid-and-dog issue for a brand-new baby. Instead I hear from parents (usually moms) shortly after the baby learns to crawl. "Suddenly" the dog begins to growl. In most cases, this surprises the parents since the dog has been "fine" with the baby for the preceding months.

All at once, everything changes. Some babies can crawl very fast (fast enough that you'd be hustling to catch them)! Now a parent's life goes from watching the baby roll back and forth on the floor to racing behind as the baby makes a beeline toward the dog's bed. Because it often seems that the dog is comfortable with the baby, many parents will allow the baby complete access to the dog, his bed, his toys, and his food, which can be a problem for the dog.

What typically happens is that the dog spends a few days leaping up and moving away from the baby, but one day either the dog feels penned in or the baby gets too close and the dog growls. Parents often see this is a betrayal of sorts. They can't believe that the dog they've loved for years is now growling at their baby when everything seemed like it was going so well.

If you are lucky, the parents, also lucky, will call at this point. But sometimes the growling isn't enough and it will take a snap (or worse, a bite) before you are called. I've had parents witness growling for months because they felt confident their dog would never bite the baby, but was "just grumbling."

As dog aficionados, one of the simplest and most effective things we can do is to tell our expectant clients about this challenging stage. If, before the baby even arrives, the parents know that they need to be more vigilant when the baby begins to crawl, they'll intervene when the baby is crawling towards the dog, rather than when he's literally crawling over the dog.

Remind the parents that with each childhood mobility milestone, things get a bit harder for the family dog. Proper supervision and management change dramatically as kids age, and parents should be prepared to make many changes over the years.

Kids & Dogs: A Professional's Guide to Helping Families

behavior, by nature, is inconsistent. Neither the dog nor the child should be faulted for that.

No Rest for the Weary

Ripley didn't adjust well to life with twins. He was always an environmentally sensitive dog and a little more high strung than many dogs. For the most part, he was gentle, comfortable, and responsive. Then the babies arrived.

Ripley's owners partitioned off a third of their dining room with an exercise pen and a crate for him. The house was small; the dining room and living room had no separation. When the babies were smaller, Ripley was allowed to hang out in the living room with everyone, but when the girls began to roll, Ripley seemed uncomfortable. He would usually head for his x-pen, and one of the parents would open the gate for him to enter.

As the girls got better at crawling, one of them developed a fascination with Ripley and his x-pen. She regularly crawled toward it and put her fingers through the wire. Ripley would move to the back. Sometimes he'd growl. The baby didn't understand his signals; she continued to approach when given the opportunity. With two crawling babies, it was hard for a supervising parent to ensure that the dog-loving baby didn't make Ripley uncomfortable in his x-pen. Several times a day, she'd get to the edge and put her fingers through. She squealed and babbled and attempted to pull herself up on the framework.

For Ripley, his x-pen didn't provide any downtime because he was the main attraction in the room. When he was trying to take a break, he still felt that a baby was pursuing him. It was harming the relationship developing between Ripley and the twins. Even though his family had tried to give him an adequate space—his area was very generous in terms of their available space—they did not give him an area where he could truly rest and recharge. We had to explore other options.

So, while I have no objection to parents physically manipulating their dog to identify potential problem areas, I caution you not to rely on any bite-prevention benefit from training a dog to accept rough handling.

While past behavior is the best predictor of future behavior, the fact that a dog has not bitten in the past does not guarantee that he will not bite in the future. Dogs grow into, not out of, aggression.

"Child-Proof" is a Misnomer

It makes me nervous when people say they want to child-proof their dog. The term implies an unrealistic guarantee on a dog's behavior regardless of the circumstances. You can child-proof kitchens and bathrooms, but not living beings.

There are many things parents can—and should—dog to make their dog safer around children, but nothing will replace careful supervision and management.

Be careful that you don't imply that there's a step-by-step plan that parents can follow to ensure that their dog never bites a child.

It's not true, it's not safe, and it's not fair.

Dog aficionados know that, but the general public does not. We need to help people understand that something that seems like a minor concern in a 7-month-old puppy might be an enormous problem when the dog is 2 years old. That's just one of the reasons why we should be encouraging people to get started in training as soon as they get their dog. The sooner they meet a qualified trainer, the better.

Caring for a dog goes way beyond scooping a bowl of kibble twice a day and scheduling an annual vet visit. Parents need to make sure that all of the dog's physical, emotional, and behavioral needs are met. Parents are busy people; therefore it can be very difficult for them to make sure that every member of their household is getting all he needs. When push comes to shove, sometimes the dog loses out.

Exercising the dog is one of the most challenging aspects of pet care for a family with young children. As we all know, it's virtually impossible to wear out

Kids & Dogs: A Professional's Guide to Helping Families

an adolescent Labrador with a 15-minute walk around the neighborhood; yet even that may be too much for some households at times. Consider a family with three children under 5. On a bright, sunny day, the mom decides to take the kids and dog for a walk. She gets the kids' jackets and shoes on and then loads the 6-month-old baby, Christopher, into the back seat of the double stroller. Two-and-a-half-year-old Lila is insisting that she wants to walk, not ride in the stroller. Ashley, 4, is pulling the front door open before Cookie is even attached to the leash. Mom scoops up Lila and straps her in the stroller, and out they go.

Fifty feet from the house, Ashley starts skipping and singing. Mom picks up the pace to keep up, and the dog is delighted. But only two houses farther, Ashley stops to watch the garbage collectors. Cookie is barking at the truck, and Mom is cajoling Ashley to come along so that they can get past the noisy truck. Christopher is tossing his toys out of the stroller. As Mom turns around to take Ashley's hand and pull her along, Lila starts insisting that she wants to walk. Mom answers, "No, no, we're going for a ride. We're going to go all the way around the block today."

Help families brainstorm ways to exercise and challenge dogs

A Tired Dog is a Well-Behaved Dog

If taking the dog out for a nice long walk or playing in the yard for 30 minutes aren't feasible daily options, get creative about finding an outlet for the dog's energy. Encourage your clients to think about giving their dogs both physical and mental outlets (and remind them that if they don't provide such outlets, the dog will come up with his own ideas, which may not be to the family's liking).

Fetch is a great way to keep a dog busy while you are concentrating on something else. You can throw a ball while sorting laundry, reading a book with the kids, putting away groceries, or talking on the phone. Throwing the ball down the stairs will require the dog to use an extra burst of energy on the return trip. (Keep a careful eye on your dog to be sure he doesn't injure himself on the stairs.)

Hide & Seek can be played with people or toys. Put the dog in a sit-stay (or have someone distract the dog) and go hide his toy, food bowl, or even yourself in another room. Encourage the dog to hunt! In addition, this is a great way to teach the dog how to find individual family members. (Do not play this game with food or toys if the dog has any resource-guarding tendencies.)

Tug-of-war can be a great calorie burner. It's not a game that I want young kids to play, but I have no objection to an adult or a teen playing a controlled game of tug with the family dog.

Playing with another dog is one of the best ways to exercise a dog. Encourage your clients to see if there's a suitable playmate for their dog in the neighborhood. Even half an hour twice a week would be a great outlet for the dogs. It's vital to find a good match though. If it's not fun for both dogs, don't do it!

Indoor obstacle courses are easy and fun. The kids can construct obstacles, or you can just take advantage of what's already there. I often move a box into a doorway and toss cheerios over it for my younger dog to retrieve. (My older dog, however, gets his treats delivered suspiciously close to wherever he is.) You can have a dog jump over a broom balanced on top of soup cans, squeeze through a narrow channel between the couch and the wall, or crawl under the coffee table. The options are limited only by your imagination, but make sure that none of your ideas will cause your dog to become frightened or stuck.

There are a great many fabulous toys too. Boomer Balls, Buster Cubes, Bob-a-lots, Squirrel Dudes, Floppy Frisbees, Chuck-its, and the always popular squeaky hedgehog. When people use toys to play with their dogs, there's a dual benefit: their relationship improves, but also the dog can sometimes learn to use the object to entertain himself.

Crates Are for Dogs, Not Kids

I often receive "cute" photos of kids and dogs together in crates. This is such a bad idea! Kids love crates. They're like play-houses and are very tempting.

Space is important to dogs, and it's vital that a dog has a spot where he can "get away from it all," knowing that he will not be disturbed. It's a parent's job to set rules that ensure that the dog's crate is not one more play area for the kids.

The next time you see a photo of a child sharing a crate with a dog, look closely at the dog's expression. It's likely you'll see toler-ance, not enjoyment.

Lila starts to cry. "Walk! I walk." Mom lifts her out, and Lila hap-pily walks along at a toddler's pace, pulling dandelions and look-ing for little rocks to pick up. After 15 minutes, they make it to the end of the street, a distance that Cookie and Mom could have cov-ered in 3 minutes if they were walking alone, and they turn around to head for home because the baby has started to fuss.

That's on a good day. Now imagine if one of the kids was sick, the weather was bad, the washer repairman had bad news, or one of the kids threw a tantrum. Not fun. No walk for Cookie on that kind of day. It's not surprising that we often see under-exercised family dogs among our clientele. It's really hard to exercise a dog when children are present. We trainers and other dog aficionados need to get creative in exercise suggestions for families. There were many times that I threw a toy down the stairs for my dog to retrieve so she could burn off a little excess energy without interfering with my kids' activities (naps, meals, or just playing happily in the living room). Older children can throw toys too, if the dog isn't one who'll bowl them over mugging for the toy.

Dogs left alone outside are at risk for being teased and becoming aggressive

Mind games and food-dispensing toys are invaluable. New toys appear on the market all the time. My long-time favorite is the Kong because it's easy to fill and dishwasher safe. Over the years, my dogs have gotten lots of table scraps stuffed into a Kong. They're happy for the treat, and I'm happy to have them actively engaged for a while. Consider a dog's possible resource-guarding issues before you recommend food-dispensing toys.

It's a considerable amount of work to manage a dog around kids, and it can seem like it would be simpler to just build a doghouse in the yard. That's a terrible idea. Dogs define "normal" as what they see all the time. The majority of dogs are comfortable with women, and most do well with men. But for many dogs, kids are scary creatures.

Children move and act very differently than adults, and in the dog world, different usually equals bad. Kids like to run through the

Kids & Dogs: A Professional's Guide to Helping Families

house, jump up and down, shriek, roll around on the floor, and slide down the stairs on their bottoms. Adults, not so much. If a dog sees children acting like children only when they come into the yard, the dog will not be comfortable with their behavior.

As a dog professional, I get Google alerts for dog bites from across the country. Far too many tell of a child being bitten after approaching a chained dog or entering a yard where a dog lives. This is completely avoidable. Social isolation does not make for good family pets. Dogs deserve to live with a family who loves them and includes them in their life.

Just because I want dogs to be fully involved in family life does not mean that I think dogs should be underfoot every minute of the day. They need downtime too! When my kids were younger, I loved naptime. It was always too short, but having a quiet time each afternoon when the kids were all in their rooms and I was reading a book on the couch was deeply restorative. Dogs also need time to recharge. Ideally, family dogs should have a place where they are able to rest undisturbed.

I like having crates with cozy beds available for dogs. If there's a comfy spot out of the action, dogs will choose to go there on their

Edzo and Gordo like to rest on cozy beds in their crates

Kong Stuffing the Easy Way

The Internet is filled with terrific ideas for stuffing Kong toys. If you have a dog that really needs a challenge, I encourage you to hunt around for some creative ideas. However, most parents stop listening when you give them an actual recipe for stuffing a Kong. "'Takes more than 1 minute? Never mind." I tend to fall in that camp myself. Occasionally I'll get inspired to stuff Kongs with exciting fillings, but on a day-to-day basis, I opt for the lazy route.

At All About Dogs, we spend a lot of time talking to people about the benefits of high-quality dog food. I definitely think good food makes a difference, so it may seem a bit surprising to reveal that one of my favorite Kong-stuffing treats is a generic dog biscuit. (Shh, don't tell the staff. They'll shoot me!) Dog biscuits are cheap, dry, and have broad ends so it's easy for me to stuff a biscuit in (without getting messy) and a bit harder for the dog to get it out.

Squeeze the Kong with your hip against the kitchen counter to elongate the larger hole—now inserting a cookie is easier! This won't keep a dog occupied for 30 minutes, but 3 minutes is enough to bring a guest in without all the canine fanfare, make a quick phone call, or keep a dog busy while the kids are getting ready for their showers.

I also think leftovers are fair game. As long as the ingredients are safe for dogs, why not put the last chicken nugget, a few green beans, or an apple slice into the Kong? That food is already cut up and ready to go . . . into the garbage disposal. Don't just feed it to the dog; have the dog work for it. At the next meal, you'll have a few more Kong-worthy morsels. Leftovers are a never-ending supply in a household with kids!

Getting a wide-mouthed funnel to scoop your dog's meal into a Kong and "seal" it with something wedged across the opening is another option. A broken dog biscuit will work.

Ready for something more "official?" Put a glob of canned pumpkin (not pumpkin mix or pie filling) in the Kong, followed by some kibble or smelly dog treats and a chunk of banana. Fill the rest of the Kong with yogurt, more canned pumpkin, or peanut butter and then freeze it. What a cool treat for the dog.

At a minimum, encourage your clients to not give the dog any leftovers unless they are in a food-dispensing toy. Even if they never discover some of the amazing Kong stuffing recipes on the Internet, you'll know that, for a few minutes every day, the dog is using his brain and having some fun. Every little bit helps.

own from time to time. Parents also have the option of crating dogs to enforce some downtime. Anytime things are too chaotic, it's okay to impose a brief period of martial law in the living room.

There are many delicious—and simple—options for stuffing food-dispensing toys

In my home, a dog in his crate must be left alone until he comes out on his own (or until I decide it is time for him to come out). Children are not allowed to bother a dog who is taking a break. This is one area where dog aficionados can help parents. Compare a dog in his crate to a toddler having a nap. Would you allow your older child to go wake up the toddler because the older child was bored? Not likely. An overtired toddler is exhausting; no parent willingly chooses to have crabby kids. Well, dogs are likely to become crabby if they're overtired too. They need to know that they can get away from the kids and have a spot that's theirs and theirs alone. It's not that parents don't care, but most have never considered that their dog needs to get completely away from their kids sometimes.

But be careful how you communicate this message to parents. If the parents feel you are judging them, they'll become defensive. I really stress the point that good dogs and good kids will have miscommunications every day. My own boys have lived with dogs since they were born, and we still have moments each day in which something could be misconstrued. Knowing what to look for and when to intervene gives parents the ability to keep everything on an even keel.

AN INTERESTING PERSPECTIVE ON FOOD

When I first started dog training, I didn't know anything beyond what I'd been taught in the basic obedience classes I had attended. I had not been exposed to the benefits of holistic treatments, body-work, food-dispensing toys, or high-quality nutrition. When people asked me about dog foods, I told them the foods sold in pet stores were better than those in the grocery store, but I didn't have any knowledge or opinion about what made a food good or bad. I had a lot to learn!

I then began to work with a trainer who knew more about food than I did. At first, it would amaze me when she would glance across the room at a bouncy puppy and say that the dog was on a low-quality food. How could she tell? We would casually bring up dog food while talking to the client and invariably find that the dog was on indeed on a low-grade food. She would recommend upgrading the dog's diet and, after only a few weeks, it was as if there was a different dog at the end of the leash. It was extraordinary—phenomenal differences in focus, attention, and ability to learn. Today the trainers on our staff quickly develop the ability to spot a dog on subpar food; it's really that profound.

One day, after a particularly trying lesson with a loopy puppy on a poor diet, one of our trainers said, "Sometimes I feel like I have it easy. I spend a lot of time managing and working with my dogs, but I'd rather have all four of them than have to live with one puppy like that. Isn't it impressive that people adopt those dogs and then work so hard with them, never realizing that it could be so much easier if the dog were on better food? These people are amazing, and they don't even know it."

Until then, I hadn't thought about it from that angle, but it's true. In many ways, our clients are working so much harder than we are, simply because they don't know some of the shortcuts to make life with a dog easier. Let's start sharing those ideas with them. The end result will be happier families and happier dogs—and may result in more dogs staying in their homes—as well as more clients for you when people start telling their friends, "Oh, you should have seen Niko before I met this great trainer, and it made all the difference."

The Third Thing Dogs Wish People Knew is . . . The Difference Between Tolerance & Enjoyment

● ● ● ● ● ● ● ● ● ● ● ● ● ● ● ● ● ● ●

One of my pet peeves is when parents proudly tell me, "My dog is great with my kids. They pull on her ears and tail, and she never does anything." That is such a hot button for me.

I find it particularly troubling that they say it with such pride. They see it as a sign that they've got a really great dog—and they most definitely do—but somehow they forget to look at the other side of the equation.

Just because your dog tolerates having her ears or tail pulled, does that make it okay? Would you allow your child to pull another child's hair? Of course not! Somehow we let things happen in kid-and-dog interactions that we'd never allow between two children.

Happy kids, tolerant dog

I attend many community events to talk with people about kids and dogs. I always hear some version of this statement. The people are proud of their dog and often tell me that they don't need to hear my presentation because they don't need any help. I take a deep breath, suppress the sarcastic comment balanced on the tip of my tongue, and start a conversation instead.

Lack of Behavior

Lack of behavior is often seen as good behavior, but there's a really important difference. We have all seen dogs who seem almost like robots: obedient and devoid of personality. These dogs impress most people, but they make me incredibly sad.

People (should) choose to have dogs in their lives because they love dogs and because they enjoy their company. From time to time, good dogs may still have typical issues, such as occasionally barking, pulling, digging, or jumping on people. Now and then, you'll encounter a dog who doesn't seem to offer much at all in terms of behavior. Watch carefully. In most cases, the dog's behaviors are suppressed.

Suppression can have a variety of causes, but the most common one is fear. When a dog is afraid (of a person's reaction, or an electric shock, or something in the environment), you may notice "lack of behavior." The dog won't show affiliative behaviors, such as loose, wiggly behavior or seeking out social contact, nor will he have an excess of canine exuberance, such as jumping on you or actively sniffing your pant leg. (Watch "The Dog Whisperer" on National Geographic with the sound turned off. You'll see many examples of suppression.)

A dog's behavior may be suppressed overall or only in certain contexts. Often the owner won't notice the lack of behavior (or will be relieved that the dog is being so "good"). It is our job—our obligation to this dog and all dogs—to point out the stress signals to the owner. When an owner can see that the dog is not "fine" in a certain circumstance, changes can be made to help the dog feel safer, more relaxed, and free to show what he's thinking and feeling. This, in turn, will make the situation safer.

I praise their dog for being so terrific and start to ask questions. How is your dog when your kids have friends over? How does he handle it when your kids wrestle? Do your kids hug him a lot? How is your dog when your baby crawls toward his bed?

Typically they'll say that the dog is "fine" with these scenarios. Listen for this word. "Fine" is not the same as "good."

I've found that people use this word when they are describing a dog who is at least a little bit uncomfort-

Fine ≠ Good

able with an interaction. For example, if asked to describe how my dogs behave when someone comes to the door, I might say they're obnoxious, delighted, excited, exuberant, or silly, but I wouldn't say they're fine. So if a client says her dog is fine when people come over, it often means the dog keeps his distance from the new person. If someone tells you his or her dog is "fine," make a note of it.

In my work with kids and dogs, I learned something that amazed me. For the most part, parents look at dog behavior as solely aggressive or non-aggressive. Aggressive is, quite obviously, bad; therefore, non-aggressive is good. Not so fast! The world of behavior is not black and white.

As dog aficionados, we could divide a dog's behavior into many different categories. In order not to overwhelm parents, though, I am lobbying for only three: Enjoyment, Tolerance, and Enough Already!

When I talk to parents about these categories, I compare them to traffic signals. A driver has to be attentive regardless of the signal, but different signals require different responses. Enjoyment is a green light, Tolerance is yellow, and Enough Already is red.

I see these behaviors as a continuum. There's a lot we can do to help a tolerant dog enjoy children more, but there's far less wiggle

Enjoyment

Things are going well. Continue supervising, but there is no need to intervene at this very moment.

Tolerance

Things are a bit tense. See what you can do to improve the situation. You may need to end the interaction.

Enough Already!

Intervene immediately. Give the kids and dogs some time apart.

room between Tolerance and Enough Already. Clearly aggression falls in the Enough Already category. Every parent knows that, but a dog consistently moving away from a child is also saying, "Enough already." That's much more subtle, but still requires the parent to take immediate action.

Teaching people the difference between tolerance and enjoyment has become one of my soapbox issues. When you ask an objective observer to decide whether a dog is enjoying an interaction, he or she usually can tell. Without any emotional entanglement, there's also no implied judgment to say that it seems the dog is only tolerating a child's attentions at this moment.

Enjoyment

Tolerance

Enough Already

Growls Are Important

It's very important not to punish a dog for giving warnings. Warnings are good! While we prefer a dog not to growl at a child, it's far better that the dog warn the parents when there is a problem than simply bite. If the dog is punished for giving warnings, his growling is suppressed. His anxiety about the situation remains, but his communication tool is lost. It's quite common to hear about dogs who bit "without warning." In most cases, the dogs' warning growls were punished and eliminated when people chastised them for "being bad."

However, it's much harder when you are emotionally involved. Seeing their four-year-old sweetly hug your dog makes most parents smile. They see the gentle, well-intentioned, affectionate gesture as a good interaction. The dog's perception is usually different. Few dogs enjoy hugs.

To tell a parent that their dog only tolerates hugs can come across as a message more about the relationship between the child and dog than an interpretation of a single interaction. You are not saying that the dog only tolerates *the child*. Be sure this is clear. Instead you are saying that the hug, however well intentioned, was not a good moment for the dog, and he merely tolerated *the hug*. Again, good kids and good dogs will have miscommunications every day. Helping parents recognize that although this is a normal part of the relationship, signs of tolerance indicate moments when they need to get involved.

As dog aficionados, we can help people shed the Good-Dog Myth (also called "The Lassie Syndrome"). Knowing that your dog is only tolerating an interaction does not make him any less of a good dog. Really. But it can feel that way, especially if someone else points out that your dog seems uncomfortable. It's tempting to interject, "he's fine." Ah, our "fine" buzzword. Yep, he's definitely not happy, content, or delighted. Just "fine." But as we said before, fine is not good.

According to Dr. Ian Dunbar, a dog can bite five times in the amount of time it takes a person with good reflexes to pull away. Parents will not be able to stop a bite that is already on its way. They will always be a moment too late. A bite is not preventable in the moment that it occurs; prevention comes through careful supervision and guidance in the many interactions that led up to it over the course of months.

Can You Move Faster Than a Dog Can Bite? Not Likely!

A dog can bite five times in the amount of time it takes a person with good reflexes to pull away.

This means that a parent cannot intervene in time to *stop* an imminent bite.

Day-to-day supervision and management *prevent* dog bites by ensuring things don't get out of hand.

Kids & Dogs: A Professional's Guide to Helping Families

The Fourth Thing Dogs Wish People Knew is . . .
Good Intentions Aren't Enough

● ● ● ● ● ● ● ● ● ● ● ● ● ● ● ● ● ●

Good intentions aren't enough. This fact is a real problem for parents. Parents spend a lot of energy thinking about dogs and infants, but later they stop worrying. We consume a lot of time worrying about how to introduce a dog to the new baby. That is usually everyone's priority. There are magazine articles, books, videos, and TV shows all focusing on that first day. Parents are understandably full of questions. How do we bring the baby home? How can we help the dog deal with the baby? Will the dog be jealous of the baby? Will the baby wake up if the dog barks? How will the dog get enough exercise when everyone is exhausted and sleep-deprived?

That first day and the weeks following, while important, are really the smallest piece of the puzzle. You have more control of the environment, the dog, and the child in the first 6 months of your child's life than you will ever have again. Yet that is what we're spending all this ink on—article after article.

If you put your baby down for a nap in a crib and close the door, the baby's still going to be there when you come back. If you put your three-year-old down for a nap and close the door, you need to hope like heck when you come back that the child is still in bed. He might be in the closet, or have opened the door, or be hanging out the window. Toddlers have terrific mobility and no sense of danger.

It's true that the first two months of a dog and child's relationship are a big adjustment period. In Karen Delise's book, *Fatal Dog Attacks*, she statistically shows that if a dog is going to kill a child,

Dogs & Storks

I believe Jen Shryock's Dogs & Storks program is the best source of information for helping a family with a dog adjust to having a baby in the house. She did an excellent job preparing her program (and continues to enhance it). For several years, people kept asking me, "Will you do a baby session?" My kids are a little bit older now, and I worried that I would neglect important points because I'm not living with young kids any more.

When I saw the Dogs & Storks program, I was pleased. I love knowing that I can pop in the DVD and have it lead me through the important points. The program keeps me on track and makes sure I don't forget anything. If you are working with expectant families, it's worth checking out: www.dogsandstorks.com.

the risk is much higher in the first two months. The dog may be thinking, "What is it? They brought it here but I'm not sure what it is." Most dogs adapt well after an initial adjustment period.

I have only seen one dog that I believed might kill the baby. It was traumatic for me. I was out of town when I got a call from a parent, and that initial conversation worried me. I made an appointment for the morning after I returned. Even though it was snowing, I did not cancel because I was so concerned about the baby. The family had two Dachshunds. They described one as really shy, but great overall. The second, however, was barky and aroused; they were worried about her behavior around the baby. I'll just call the dogs Shy and Barky. When my business partner, Robin Bennett, and I arrived, Shy and Barky both hated us, but Shy—the dog they weren't worried about—was really reactive toward the baby. She was trying to scale her way into the playpen. She seemed predatory to us. At one point, while the father was holding the infant, Shy leaped to bite the foot of the sleeper the baby was wearing.

Fortunately, the sleeper was a bit too large for the baby, so the dog only got a mouthful of cloth. The father was used to Shy jumping, didn't realize she'd gotten hold of the sleeper and didn't react. The mother saw Shy bite the fabric, but still, the two of them were more worried about Barky. Barky was, as described, barky and aroused. I suspected they'd have trouble with her when the baby began to crawl, but Shy was a problem right this instant. Yet the parents didn't see it! Robin and I had to tell them that we were afraid to leave their home because we were worried about the baby's safety.

The clients were not thrilled with me. I tried really hard to say it nicely and talk about the management they could do and the ways we could help. I recommended double management everywhere. Before we left, Shy actually managed to get into the playpen! Fortunately, the baby was not in it at the time. The dog just kept leaping until she got in. Frightening.

The scene terrified me. Afterward, Robin and I stood outside in the snow talking about the situation. The parents didn't understand our deep concern that their "good dog" was behaving dangerously aggressively toward their child.

The dog didn't kill the baby, thank God. (We lost contact with the client after a few months, so I don't know how things went during the crawling stage.) I'd never seen a dog like that before, and I hope I never will again. The odds of actually

Not everyone will be delighted to have a new baby in the house

seeing this situation before a bite are low because such cases so rare.

If you are ever watching a dog interact with a baby and your stomach drops, you have a responsibility to those parents to say, "I've been doing this for many years, and I've had situations I've worried about and stressed over, but this is out of the ordinary. I am afraid to leave your home because I'm worried about your baby's safety." You have to say it.

That said, most families cruise through the first few months. They congratulate themselves on how well their dog has adapted to life with a baby and believe that the dog loves the baby as much as they do. And then life gets more difficult, and everyone is caught by surprise. When people are expecting a child, people ask, "How do you think Buddy's going to handle it?" They talk about it. But when your baby learns to crawl, few people think to ask, "How's Buddy handling things now?" They don't. You've made it through that first introduction. You did it properly; so now life is good, isn't it?

We have to be clear and tell parents about the challenges ahead. We need to be cheerleaders on the sidelines saying, "You can do it. It's going to get more complicated, but you're going to gain experience every day. You're going to be up to the challenge of managing kids and dogs. We know that you love Buddy. Learning how to set him up for success with your kids is one of the kindest things you can do for him. That way he'll know that you are always there to help if he needs it."

We have to do it in a way that does not sound as if we are suggesting they have a bad kid or a bad dog, but doing that is harder than it sounds. Parents are very sensitive to anyone implying that they aren't doing a good job. If we make the parents defensive, they won't listen.

To circumvent those defenses, consider taking a sympathetic approach. Try saying something like, "I can't imagine what you go

How Can I Help with the New Baby?

Encourage all of your expectant clients to make a list of ways that friends and family members can help them when their baby arrives. People want to help. Let them!

✔ Stuff several Kongs and put them in the freezer.

✔ Purchase a copy of *Living with Kids and Dogs . . . Without Losing Your Mind* for the parents and the grandparents.

✔ Watch the baby so one or both of the parents can walk or play with the dog.

✔ Walk the dog for 30 minutes.

✔ Scoop the yard.

✔ Take the dog to the groomer or vet as needed.

✔ Keep the dog for a weekend.

✔ Play fetch with the dog.

✔ Help arrange furniture so the dog has plenty of escape routes when the baby starts to crawl.

✔ Purchase a crate and train the dog to enjoy using it.

✔ Provide bully sticks or pig's ears so the dog can have some dedicated chewing time each day (if there are no resource-guarding issues).

✔ Make a conscious effort to ask about the dog, not just when the baby is born, but always. Parents may have concerns that friends and family can help address.

Visit www.livingwithkidsanddogs.com to download this list as a hand-out for your clients.

through every morning trying to get breakfast together. Maybe we can work on mat training so you could make breakfast and Buddy wouldn't approach the table," or "I wonder how it would be if we gave him a stuffed Kong in his crate or behind a baby gate while the kids ate?"

Our message has to be, "You're doing great, but let's do even better." If we imply they're doing it all wrong, we'll lose the client, which won't help the dog at all. It's a balancing act.

EXPECTATIONS

Somewhere, at this very moment, a child is jumping over the family dog and no one is telling the child to stop. In fact, the parent may well be videotaping this seemingly adorable interaction. (YouTube has many, many videos that I find alarming in which a child is doing something with the family dog, under parental supervision, such as it is, that no dog aficionado would ever recommend.)

But I Meant It Nicely...

Good intentions are not enough. We have all had the experience of someone misinterpreting something we said innocently. When that happens, even though we had no ill intent, we owe the other person an apology because our meaning was misconstrued and may have caused hurt feelings.

Similarly, just because your child is feeling affectionate and is "sharing" his blanket with the dog, the dog may not be happy with the interaction. It's imperative that we consider not only the child's intentions, but also the dog's response. If either the dog or the child is not happy (we need more than just tolerance), then a parent should get involved to either help everyone enjoy the interaction or end it quickly.

Parents don't really have a good understanding of what is fair or unfair. For some reason, dogs fall in the "safe" category—things we don't have to worry about. This mystifies me. When a child crawls toward the top of a staircase or reaches for an electrical socket, a parent rushes to intervene. If the child is poking the dog in the eye, however the parent may just tell the child to stop—without any sense of urgency.

When this happens, people let down their dogs. Believing they have the most wonderful dog in the entire universe, they will allow him to be harassed daily for the rest of his life. Harassed with good intentions, but harassed nonetheless. It's not cute and it's not fair, and it's imperative we help people understand that.

The very first mistake that parents make is encouraging their children to show affection to the dog in ways that are not necessarily kind to the dog. We believe that if an action is intended to be kind, then it is kind, but that's not always true. I have a friend who's very afraid of dogs. She was determined not to make her children afraid of dogs. A few years ago, she visited my house with her 2-year-old son. At the time, I had only one dog, Gordo, who is the world's best napper. He excels at sleeping. My friend was very nervous about being around my dog. So we sat in the kitchen, visited, and talked with her son. He was climbing up and down on a kitchen chair, and my dog was sleeping. It was all good. Then, when it was time to leave, she said, "Okay, Michael, give Gordo a hug goodbye." I was stunned. I reminded her, "Uh, remember you are the one afraid of dogs? Remember how you were not breathing when you came in and now you're telling your child to go squeeze someone else's dog? Oh my!"

My dog would have tolerated a hug well, but it wasn't an appropriate thing to do to a dog, so I didn't allow it. My friend is a smart person and a good parent. As someone who's actively trying not to create a fearful child, she told her child to do something dangerous because she thought it was a nice thing to do. She didn't realize that what she was suggesting was dangerous.

Instead, she had decided after spending 2 hours with my lethargic dog, the dog was safe and that it would be okay for her child to give the dog a hug on his way out the door. But while it would have been okay with Gordo, it would not have been a good thing to teach her child. It would not have been something that dog aficionados would encourage, but in a similar situation, I bet most of our clients would have allowed Michael to hug their dog. That's where

Gordo cuddling with Brandon

we come in. As dog aficionados, we're always having to educate people, bit by tiny bit.

We need to ask ourselves, does this dog actually adore this child? It's a really tricky thing. Some dogs really love children. I didn't know much about kids and dogs when I had my first child. Though I had taken many training classes with various dogs over the years, I actually taught my first class right when I got pregnant. These two events occurred in close succession, and I think that it played a role in why I wrote *Living with Kids and Dogs*. I'm a voracious reader, so I read every childcare book and every dog book available because I knew I had a lot to learn about both. I wasn't able to find much good information about on managing kid-and-dog interactions. As luck would have it, I had a lovely dog who adored my children. I was not a brilliant person who did a great job managing every interaction. I didn't; I did not know how to manage. I would have loved some advice from a dog aficionado.

There was one incident when my dog, Midas, growled at my son, and I handled it completely wrong. Midas was lying with her back against the couch, when he crawled over and then up on her! She growled, and I had a parental freak-out. I scooped Justin up and said, "Go away!" to her. She went about 8 feet away, probably wondering what the heck had happened.

An hour later, when I was able to look back more rationally, I chastised myself up about it. My child was approaching my dog, and I was watching and thinking it was cute. I wasn't watching for any stress signals or checking to see if Midas had an easy escape route. I was supposed to be her advocate, but instead I was an idiot who let a situation get to a growling point. And then worse, I punished Midas for communicating her discomfort in the only way she could.

Similar incidents happen everyday in an untold number of households. There are 19 million American families with kids and dogs—19 million! There are many people to whom we need to get this information. Some dogs love people; some dogs don't. Some dogs love kids; some dogs don't. There's no way for us to communicate to a dog what it means to have a baby join the family. We just expect a dog to think, "Cool, a baby!"

People don't understand that having an infant arrive is going to change this dog's world for the rest of his life. The dog is not going to understand every change (or perhaps any of them), so it's the owner's responsibility to acknowledge, "Okay, this is a little weird, but let's try to make it easier for you by giving you more doggy things to do to help you adjust to these changes" or otherwise giving the dog the support he needs.

Dogs are put in a tricky position. They are considered part playmate and part nanny. My definition of family includes my dogs, and probably yours does too, doesn't it? Your pets are your family. But what sometimes happens is we get this convoluted equation that doesn't add up.

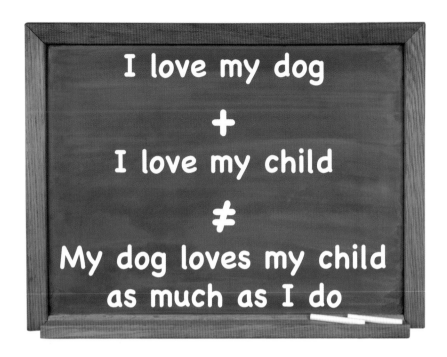

I love my dog

+

I love my child

≠

My dog loves my child
as much as I do

I have three sons, and I love them all. They love each other too, but they get on each other's nerves a lot. That's perfectly normal. I wish I could tell you that each of my boys finds his brothers so charming that he's always kind and gentle, patient and supportive, loving and generous. It's a lovely fantasy, but not very realistic. Each of them is a normal kid who often finds his brothers annoying. Most parents, including my husband and me, don't have a problem with that.

So why do expect our dogs to do better than our kids? We expect dogs to be as tolerant and affectionate toward our children as we are—and sometimes even more so, because we adults are allowed to show when we are annoyed with them. We don't allow our dogs to do even that.

We expect the dogs not only to be more tolerant than we are, but also to be that way with no help from us. I sometimes show a video of a dog named Daisy playing with a squeaky toy. The baby is interested in the toy and grabs it while the dog is still holding on.

Important Conversation with a Dog

This how I imagine expectant parents would break the news to their dog, if only the dog could understand . . .

"You know we love you, Buddy. You are the most wonderful dog ever. We have some exciting news we want to share with you. We're going to have a baby! A baby is like a human puppy. Puppies are cute, right? Well, except for my sister's puppy who pesters you all the time—oh, and that new terrier puppy on the corner—but mostly you like puppies, don't you?

"We know our baby is going to love playing with you . . . in about a year and a half. She won't be able to play with you for a while. In fact, we won't be able to play with you as much either. We're going to be really busy taking care of the baby.

"She'll probably cry a lot, but you don't need to worry. We'll take care of her. She'll also have lots of new stuff in the house. You can sniff it, but please don't chew anything! And all those new fleecy toys are for the baby. I know they have squeakers and smell ter-rific, but, really, they are baby toys. Leave them alone.

"We'll still love you just as much as always, but there will be a few new rules. You might not get to sit on the couch any more, and we really don't want you paw-ing us for attention when we hold the baby. Also, could you please stop barking at those squirrels? We won't want you to wake up the baby when she's sleeping.

"Isn't this exciting? We know you are just going to love having a baby in the family!"

Golden Dogs?

I use a lot of videos in my presentations. I think it's telling that many of the videos have Golden Retrievers interacting with babies and toddlers. Golden Retrievers have the reputation of being the perfect family dog. A couple gets married and hopes to have kids

one day, but not yet. In the meantime, they'd love to have a dog, but they want a dog that will be good with those future children. So they get a Golden Retriever. And then when the kids come, they don't worry about anything because "everyone knows Golden Retrievers love kids." But try telling that to the dog in this picture.

That view is too simplistic. There are many Goldens who would not be happy living with kids. People should choose a dog based on his temperament, not his breed, and super-socialize the dog with babies and children if they are planning to have a family. Remember that every dog—regardless of breed or sociability—needs someone who is watching to make sure all interactions are gentle, kind, and welcome.

Initially, the mother is charmed. She coos, "Daisy's playing. Daisy's a good girl." But when the baby is nearly tipped over as Daisy tugs gently on the toy, suddenly the mother's voice becomes more harsh, "Daisy! DAISY!" The mother was stressed because Daisy did not figure out on her own that the child was about to tip over.

What was the matter with Daisy? Well, first of all, she was a dog, and second, it was her squeaky toy. It's very unreasonable to expect a dog to always self-handicap when playing with a child. Why don't parents intuitively understand that? Because they just haven't actually sat down and considered what they are asking the dog to do. If we can get people to think about what we are asking the dog to do and whether the dog needs more assistance to reach our expectations, we'll be doing a great public service.

I have a video clip of a 1-year-old petting her dog. She begins by petting the dog's back, but soon moves toward his face. Her mom, who is videotaping, continually praises the dog. When the girl pokes the dog in the eye for the third time, the mom says, "That's his eye, Sophie!" She reaches out to move her daughter's hand away from the dog's eye, but doesn't make any attempt to move the child away from the dog or otherwise change the interaction. Poor dog.

The mother thinks she's teaching her child to love dogs. But she's also teaching her dog to not love kids. The dog is wonderful. He accepts the petting without trying to move away, but he's clearly not happy. The fact that the mom videotaped it tells me this happens over and over again. Well…that's not okay. Sophie is being, in her mother's opinion, kind to the dog. Because the gesture was intended kindly, the parent did not intervene.

So when a child decides that she loves her dog so much that she wants to make him a Halloween costume that he can wear for the next six months every time she thinks of it, she means it nicely, so the mom says, "Okay, great, you can do that," while the dog is thinking, "Oh, no! The cape, it's coming again."

Few dogs enjoy costumes

We have to help people to see that just because you meant well doesn't mean you were kind, and that's a challenge for people. On www.livingwithkidsanddogs.com,

I've got three short videos that show people expressing affection in human ways:

- ➤ Hugging a dog
- ➤ Kissing a dog
- ➤ Patting a dog on the head

These are three common ways people show affection to dogs, and, in most cases, the dogs don't like it. We show these videoclips in our orientation for basic obedience classes. We talk a little bit about dog body language and how to tell the difference between Enjoyment, Tolerance, and Enough Already. By showing these videos and pointing out some stress signals, we can illustrate that just because we intended something kindly, it does not necessarily make it kind.

But we also have to deliver a balanced message. We certainly don't want our students asking, "You mean our dogs don't even like us?" That's not our message at all. Instead we want our clients to see that our dogs are attempting to communicate with us at all times, and that by knowing a little bit about body language, the clients can interact in ways that make dogs comfortable and recognize when their dogs are uncomfortable.

We especially want to teach parents about these three forms of misconstrued affection: hugs,

You Can Make a Difference

Through gentle education and teachable moments, dog aficionados encourage people to become more aware, to watch more, to intervene more, and to do better. We are not going to reach perfection. Ever.

Let's just throw that idea out the window and instead focus on helping all of your clients to do a little bit better than they were doing before they met you. When they are more aware, they will try harder and they will do better. That alone will make phenomenal differences in dogs' lives and bite statistics.

kisses, and head pats. However, it's important to know that just because you've told them doesn't mean the behavior will end.

After all, how many of us still hug and kiss our dogs? I do, every day. I know my dogs don't really like it, but I love them so much that I often communicate my feelings in a very human way. The difference is that, because I know that the dogs are just tolerating my enthusiasm, I watch for stress signals and keep things low key enough that the dogs aren't really bothered by my rude attempts at affection.

Twenty years ago, no clients said, "I want to socialize my dog." Now clients do. We've gotten the word out there. Do people understand what socialization is? No, they think it means throw your puppy into the dog park and let the big dogs play with him. That's not quite what we meant—but owners are starting to understand the concept and are trying to apply it. At least they know that socialization is important, and they ask about it when they talk to trainers and other dog aficionados.

If we spend time teaching people to look for tolerance versus enjoyment and to recognize that their dog is communicating all the time, they're not going to get it right all the time, but they're at least going to know that it exists. And they may get it right some or even most of the time.

Most serious bites come from adult male dogs, between 2 and 5 years old. The bite statistics drop off sharply after 5 years of age. It's not because dogs become nicer. It's because either people get a lot better at managing their dog or else the dog is euthanized, rehomed, or relinquished to a shelter.

Children between 5 and 9 are bitten more than any other group of people, and boys are bitten twice as often as girls. When I talk with parents about safety, I say that if dog bites were unpredictable, we would not be able to distinguish bite victims by age or sex. A dog would randomly bite and the damage would be evenly spread throughout the population.

The fact that bites are not random gives us more power to prevent them. In the vast majority of bites, the dog and the child are familiar with each other. This is not what parents think. Parents honestly believe that their dog would never ever bite their child or anyone else's child. Instead, they worry about a loose strange dog or the sweet, friendly American Pit Bull Terrier who lives up the street.

We have to get people to think differently. Instead of devoting all of our resources to planning how to introduce the dog to the baby, we should focus more on what may happen in the years that follow babyhood. If we do the math, we know that kids are most at risk for a dog bite between the ages of 5 and 9 and that most biting dogs are between 2 and 5. Therefore, when a family dog bites a child, in most cases it's not the dog who was so carefully introduced to the baby. It's the next dog. Think about it.

We focus so much time and energy helping the first dog adjust to living with the baby. Then that dog lives out his natural lifespan, or we decide to add a dog to the household. The next dog moves into a house with bigger kids, and then we have all sorts of management issues. Older children are more active and the less super-

This dog is showing stress signals

Parents want happy kids and happy dogs

vised. It's just reality. When people say, never ever leave a child alone in a room with a dog, you have to wonder… how are you going to do that every day for the rest of your life?

Imagine this scenario: You are in the front hall, strapping the baby into her portable car seat. Your seven-year-old already has his jacket on and you ask him to grab your purse and the keys. Are you really going to say, "Oh wait, those are in the dining room. Don't go yet. I need to go with you to get them because the dog might see you there?"

Meanwhile, your four-year-old is yelling, "I can't find my shoes." You say, "They're in your room. Go get them. Hurry up!" So your four-year-old goes up the stairs alone to get his shoes, the seven-year-old goes to get the purse from the dining room, you're still strapping the baby into the car seat in the hallway. Where's the dog? Hopefully right next to you. Great. But let's say you have three dogs. Are they all next to you? Every minute of every day for the rest of those dogs' lives?

Parents can't manage life to that extreme. They will send the four-year-old upstairs to find his shoe or tell a six-year-old to go turn off the kitchen light. If we say to parents that they can't ever have a child step out of their sight, they'll think, "Those dog people are crazy; they don't get it." And they'd be right.

We have to meet parents in the middle. We need to make sure that their children know how to interact with dogs, we need to make sure their dogs are safe with children, and we need to make sure we're mitigating their risks, so that when the child goes up the stairs as the dog comes down, nothing bad is going to happen in the middle.

That is day-to-day reality. Over and over, nothing happens in the middle. So while bites are frightening and the statistics are scary, let's keep in mind that less than 1 percent of dog bites need medical attention. Family dogs have endless opportunities to hurt children, but rarely do. We need people to know, "Yes, your dog is a saint, but saints need help too." There will be frequent miscommunications; let's just acknowledge that reality and proceed from there.

The Fifth Thing Dogs Wish People Knew is . . .
What to Look For & When to Intervene

● ● ● ● ● ● ● ● ● ● ● ● ● ● ● ● ● ●

In many cases, the only kid-and-dog advice a parent gets is "never leave a child and a dog alone together." If only it were that easy. My files are filled with stories of children bitten when an adult was nearby. These adults believed they were supervising, but since no one taught them what to look for and when to intervene, they missed (or dismissed) many early signs of impending trouble.

Imagine that you stopped by the hospital to visit a critically ill friend and the ICU nurse said, "I'm going to take my lunch break. Just keep an eye on those monitors, and yell if you need me." Without training, how would you know which numbers were worrisome and which had considerable fluctuation while still in the normal range? You wouldn't. If anything happened to your friend, you'd be left saying, "I'm so sorry. I didn't know."

Although they don't know it, parents are in a similar position. Supervising kid-and-dog interactions is hard work! Unfortunately most parents don't think so. They're wearing rose-colored glasses because they love their dog and are absolutely sure that he would never bite a child. They fervently believe that . . . until the moment their dog actually bites.

Nobody is teaching parents *how* to supervise. Think of all those articles about introducing a new baby to the family dog. How many have useful, concrete advice? Most give guidelines so vague that parents don't feel they apply to their situation or to their dog.

That's where we come in. Dog aficionados are uniquely qualified to teach parents how to supervise. If we take the time to teach all

dog owners a few common stress signals and tell them that these signals are caution signs that require them to take action, we'll have people intervening before things get too stressful—and before the relationship between the child and the dog is damaged.

A dog's only method of communicating is body language. A dog tries to tell us what we need to know. Unfortunately, people don't recognize the signals a dog sends, so many valuable canine messages get lost in transmission. Consequently, a person can believe that a dog bit without warning, while the dog actually gave multiple warnings—but no one listened.

Entire books have been written about dog body language. As dog aficionados, we find them fascinating, but our clients may not share that opinion. It's easy to give someone too much information. When that happens, they become overwhelmed and tune us out. I believe it's far superior to give clients a short list of easily identifiable signals, preferably with photos. The photos make it much easier for people to understand what you are talking about. The seven signals I emphasize are a closed mouth, turning away, lip licking, half-moon eye, shaking off, yawning, and breathing changes.

Be sure to emphasize that these are not signs of aggression, but instead are signals that, if not heeded, may lead to aggression.

Closed Mouth

I sometimes joke that if I had to give a 5-second dog-bite prevention lecture, I would say, "If the dog's mouth is closed, leave him alone. Problem solved." That's flippant, but also pretty accurate.

When people are tense, they usually close their mouths. It's a behavior driven by the limbic system, which is the center for emotions. A dog isn't thinking, "Hmm, I'm a little uncomfortable, so I'll close my mouth now." It just happens. This is an important sign to know.

Show this picture of the Shelties to anyone over the age of 4 and ask which dog is happier. You'll get the correct answer 95 percent of the time. However, people won't necessarily know how they knew that the dog lying down was less comfortable than the other dog. Point out how much a small detail, such as a closed mouth, can change a dog's appearance. It's a subtle signal, but the effect and meaning are dramatic.

Both dogs are looking at the same thing, but the bottom dog is more nervous about it

Turning Away

When we enjoy interacting with someone, we turn toward him or her, but when we've "had enough," we turn away. As kids and dogs are often moving around while a parent watches from the couch, it's easy to just see movement without noting direction. Encourage parents to pay attention to whether the dog is approaching the child or spending

Turning away

more time moving away. If the dog is consistently moving away from the child, a parent should redirect the child's focus and, if necessary, give the dog some downtime in another room.

Be certain that the dog always has at least two escape routes because, at any given time, a child or a large toy may block one of them. (Preschool toys are enormous!) Knowing that he can move away will help a dog maintain a lower stress level.

Lip Licking

Lip licking

I think lip licking is the canine equivalent of thumb sucking. Children use thumb sucking as a self-soothing activity, and it's more common in slightly stressful situations. Looking at it in that light, it's easy to see that an increase in lip licking indicates that the dog is feeling somewhat stressed and would appreciate adult assistance.

Half-Moon Eye

Half-moon eye

A relaxed dog does not typically show the whites of his eyes. (Snub-faced or bulging-eyed dogs are the exception.) The half-moon effect is the result of facial tension. Half-moon eye is an easily identifiable signal; you either see it or you don't. If you see it, find a way to lower the stress or arousal. (Note: Sometimes also called "whale eye.")

Shaking Off

I strongly believe there's a neurological reset that occurs when the body is shaken. When an athlete is knocked down, the coach will tell him to "shake it off." Similarly, if I bite into something tart, I'm likely to rapidly shake my head back and forth until the sensation dies down.

When you see a dry dog shake off, take note. Something stressful just happened. A shake off usu-

Shaking off

ally occurs after the stressful moment has passed, but it provides valuable information. If a dog consistently shakes off after a child drives a remote-control car down the hall, the parent should either suggest a different route or ensure the dog moves to a more restful spot.

Yawning

Yawning

My Tellington Touch (TTouch) friends tell me that dogs hold their tension in their jaws, hind legs, and tails. Sometimes, a yawn indicates only sleepiness, but more often than not, it seems to be a way of relieving tension in the jaw.

Think of how tight your jaw becomes during a stressful day. Watch people in traffic. You'll see a lot of people stretching their neck or popping their jaw.

A dog's yawn is typically combined with turning away from the source of stress. It's always worth noting when a dog turns away from someone and yawns, especially if the person is a child. Being tired of something or someone is different from just being tired. Once parents learn this distinction, they'll be better able to keep things safe and fun between their kids and their dog.

Breathing Changes

I love clear-cut signals such as a closed mouth, turning away, lip licking, half-moon eye, shaking off, and yawning, but I also think it's valuable to point out a dog's breathing changes to owners. Most people don't pay attention to their dog's breathing. Why would they? It's just a basic physical requirement, right? But dog aficionados know that a dog's breathing pattern can give us clues about his emotional state.

In our Relaxing Rowdy Rovers class, dog-aggressive dogs work behind barriers before venturing out into the open area. Often a dog who performs beautifully in his "condo" will pant noisily when we bring him out into the open. I point this out to the owners. It is not hotter in the center of the room, it's *harder*. Dogs pant when they are stressed. Conversely, a stressed dog may hold his breath. Whenever someone brings a dog to my kids' sporting events, I keep an eye on the dog's breathing. Most dogs will either pant or hold their breath when a group of unfamiliar kids approaches to say hi. I have yet to see an owner respond to these changes, but I keep hoping.

This dog is holding his breath

This all goes back to good moment/bad moment, not good dog/bad dog. Every dog will have some bad moments, as do we. Our challenge as dog aficionados is to help parents recognize these non-aggressive signals as something important enough to act upon. Waiting for the dog to show overt signs of aggression will make it much harder for you to remedy the kid-and-dog relationship.

These seven signals can serve as useful warnings. Dogs know how to recognize them in other dogs and will typically modify their own behavior to alleviate the other dog's stress. But most people don't know that these behaviors have any meaning. Consequently, dogs often feel the need to use more overt signals (stiffening, growling, snarling, or snapping) in stressful situations with people.

Unfortunately, once a dog has progressed to more serious signals, the dog typically starts at that level in future incidents. For example, if no one intervenes when a dog repeatedly lip licks or turns away from a child, eventually the dog may growl. In that case, a parent will usually intervene. The dog then learns that nothing less than a growl is effective. You can expect more growling in the future.

We did an evaluation of a 7-year-old dog named Hanna who lived with 21- and 6-month-old boys. Hanna had begun growling at the older boy. James was becoming very mobile and loved to follow Hanna around. When he would get close to Hanna, she would growl at him, especially if she was resting on the couch. By the time they came to our office, Hanna had been growling at James for a few months and the mother wanted to know if I thought Hanna would "get over it." Her perception was that Hanna liked the younger son and had previously liked James, but, for some reason, didn't any longer.

When I describe Hanna's behavior to dog aficionados, they correctly surmise that James' mobility was Hanna's biggest issue. It wasn't that Hanna liked him better when he was little; he was just easier to avoid. Now that he could get around—and because his mother was often busy with the baby—James was interacting with Hanna a lot more than Hanna was comfortable with. So she was growling. Every day.

Hanna had not bitten James. Yet. When we watched him interact with her in our office, she showed all seven of the signals listed,

Enough Already: the dog is moving away from the child

Kids & Dogs: A Professional's Guide to Helping Families

but never growled. The parents were shocked to see how many times Hanna expressed her discomfort without showing any signs of aggression because they believed Hanna growled unpredictably. I have a videoclip in which James is sitting on the floor near his mom and Hanna is standing open-mouthed looking at her. The moment James puts his hands on the floor to hoist himself up, Hanna's mouth closes. She stops breathing, turns away, and then moves rapidly out of his way. Those behaviors, which never meant anything to James's parents before, suddenly became very revealing.

UNDERSTANDING THE SIGNALS

It is imperative that we keep in mind that parents are doing the best they can with what they know. It will not help for us to give impassioned speeches about safe and kind child-and-dog interactions if we only succeed in making the parents defensive about their home lives. Even offering regular community education about kids and dogs isn't very effective because most parents don't think they have a problem, and therefore they don't show up. (Although they may be convinced that their neighbor or sister-in-law really needs to see such a presentation, they usually have no such concerns about their own household!)

When you know better, you do better. As dog aficionados, we can easily add canine body language to the list of things we teach. Not necessarily in lecture format, but in an unknown number of tiny observations in our classes and private lessons. It's vital, though, that we be careful with our word choices. We must not appear to be beating people over the head or berating them for not knowing the very things that we have spent years learning about. If we all make an effort to share our observations, a little at a time, people will learn that their dog's behavior has meaning and context. This knowledge will help people to advocate for their dogs and set them up for success.

As dog owners learn about canine stress signals, they have a responsibility to act on them. From a canine perspective, Halloween is my least favorite holiday. In fact, years ago, my family decreed

How to Get Parents to Come to Community Events

I don't think lectures are the best way to help parents make lasting changes in their households, but they can be a way to get the word out about your services. I do a variety of community-service presentations each year. For the most part, they are poorly attended. Sixty people will sign up for a lecture on reactive dogs or alternative therapies; yet I'm lucky to get a dozen or so interested in hearing about kids and dogs. Few people think there's a problem in their own home.

I am determined not to be Chicken Little shouting "danger, danger," but I admit it's frustrating to have people tell me that they don't need to hear my presentation because their dog is great with kids. After all, she lets them climb all over her, and she never does anything. Oh dear.

I've tried a variety of ways to generate interest without much success. Recently I came up with a new blurb that I am excited about. I hope it will pique some people's interest and get more folks to attend my annual workshop for a local nonprofit organization. Here's the blurb—if you borrow it, don't print the parts in brackets in your flyer.

Take This Quick Quiz about Kids & Dogs

1. **Name three things a dog does with his mouth that indicate discomfort.** [Closed mouth, yawning, lip licking]

2. **Which age group receives the most dog bites: kids from 0-5, 5-9, or 9-13?** [5-9]

3. **Golden Retrievers, Greyhounds, and Labrador Retrievers share one trait that can make supervision trickier. What is it? (Many other popular breeds have this trait as well.)** [They're known as tolerant dogs, and because they tolerate a lot, parents often don't intervene when they should.]

4. **Name the three categories of dog behavior that all parents need to know.** [Enjoyment, Tolerance, and Enough Already]

5. **What are three common signs of human affection that make dogs uncomfortable?** [Hugging, kissing, and patting on the head]

I am hoping to get people wondering what the answers to the questions are and willing to spend an hour to come listen to a free presentation to learn more. It's a new idea, so I don't know yet how effective it will be, but I'm excited to try it. If you have a great idea for gathering a crowd without using fear tactics, I'd love to hear it!

Kids & Dogs: A Professional's Guide to Helping Families

that I should stay home passing out candy, rather than accompany my kids around the neighborhood because I dampened everyone's enthusiasm by worrying aloud about the dogs I'd see barking behind screen doors or walking warily past caped crusaders! Most dogs hate Halloween, but many people enjoy including their unsuspecting dogs in the festivities. If we can help them look objectively at their dog's behavior, they'll see that certain activities—while fun for people—are definitely not fun for dogs. Once they gain that understanding, hopefully they will be less inclined to put their dog in those sorts of situations.

For parents, this means that the list of seven common stress signals should serve as calls to action. These signals indicated that it's time to intervene before your child gets hurt and your dog is banished. Act now. If you wait, it may be too late.

Guidelines

It is impossible to write a one-size-fits-all set of guidelines for child-and-dog interactions. Patricia McConnell jokes that she'd like to write a book called "It Depends" because that's her answer to so many behavioral queries. She's right! Dog behavior is complex, and if you add in all the variables related to children, "it depends" is the one and only honest answer.

I currently have two dogs. One is much more sensitive than the other. I watch my kids' interactions with Edzo carefully because he worries far more about loud noises, abrupt movements, and scary body language than Gordo does. Edzo shows stress signals in situations that Gordo thinks are just raucous fun. By knowing that stress signals indicate a need for change, my kids can play with both dogs in ways that please all of them.

For children 6 and under, I encourage parents to think about what they'd allow their child to do with a 6- to 8-month-old baby. Would you allow your child to carry the baby from room to room? Play alone with the baby? Pull the baby's leg when he's crawling? Take a toy away from the baby? You'd be right there supervising your

Discourage children from carrying dogs

child interacting with that baby, and you should be there when the child is playing in the company of a dog too.

I never let kids under 10 carry another child (regardless of age) and similarly, I don't believe that children should carry dogs. Many dogs learn to wiggle and snap just so they'll be put down on the ground. We don't want the dogs rehearsing that behavior, nor do we want children to think it's okay to carry a dog around like a toy.

Parents can usually tell when one child is causing another child stress. They'll step in to smooth things over. Unfortunately, I've found that parents typically have no idea when their child is causing a dog stress, so they don't intervene.

MANAGEMENT

Often it's easier to prevent a problem than to be perpetually vigilant. Parents quickly learn to keep crayons out of sight when it's not time for coloring. Electrical sockets are capped, cabinets are locked, and dangerous liquids are stored safely away from children.

Kaitlyn's Dog-Bite Story

Kaitlyn, 8, came to one of our kids-and-dogs camps. We were talking about situations that we'd handle differently now that we know more about dogs. Most of the kids told about a dog chasing them or jumping on them. Kaitlyn's story began, "I had a friend . . . I have a friend who was bitten by my dog." That one sentence pulls my heartstrings because she's lucky enough that the other girl's parents allowed the friendship to continue. If your dog bites someone else's child, the friendship is usually over. Kaitlyn feels very guilty for something that is not her fault, but the good news is that she still has her friend.

Kaitlyn had a chow/terrier mix named Reilly who was okay with her, but very uncomfortable with other kids—actually strangers of any age. When I met Reilly at our office, he stared intently at me and focused on every movement. He did not solicit any attention, and I was very cautious around him. However, at home, his family just told guests to leave Reilly alone. They didn't take special precautions. Reilly had growled at many people, but had never bitten anyone—and they believed he never would. Many people are under the mistaken impression that a growl comes in lieu of a bite.

One day, Kaitlyn had a classmate over. They sat at the kitchen table eating ice cream and talking with Kaitlyn's father. Reilly watched them from across the room. When the girls finished eating, they got up to carry their bowls to the dishwasher. Kaitlyn passed by Reilly without incident, but when her friend tried to walk by him, Reilly jumped up and bit her face. He tore her bottom lip, and she needed to get stitches. (The location of the bite is not surprising. Seventy-seven percent of dog bites to children are on the face.)

The incident occurred even though Kaitlyn's father was in the same room. Supervision of kid-and-dog interactions requires much more involvement than never leaving a dog and a child alone together. After meeting Reilly, I asked the family a lot of questions about his behavior. He had never shown any sociability toward anyone outside the family, but because he had never shown overt aggression toward a stranger, Kaitlyn's father didn't think to put Reilly in another room when Kaitlyn had a friend over. He made the common mistake of thinking of behavior as only aggressive (bad) and non-aggressive (good) rather than looking for Enjoyment, Tolerance, and Enough Already because he didn't know otherwise.

Dog owners employ a lot of management too. Leashes keep dogs safe on walks, baby gates or closed doors keep them out of certain rooms, and counters are kept clear to discourage counter-surfing. Living with kids and dogs takes management to a whole new level! As dog aficionados, we need to be open to new ideas because every household will have special circumstances that need to be considered. Our primary goal is to educate the parents about the level of supervision needed and then supplement their game plan with ideas of our own. The parents know more about the special needs of their child, their dog, and their home, so it's crucial for you to incorporate their ideas into your management plan.

Things to Consider

- Double up on management, especially with dogs who have behavioral concerns.

- Have a comfortable, safe place for the dog to be away from the kids—one that the dog can get to without help as well as one in a different room where the dog can be blocked in or out with a closed door or baby gate.

- Create escape routes. Family rooms get crowded with children's toys; so move the plastic pirate ship out of the dog's getaway route! There need to be at least two escape options— regardless of where the dog and child are—so if the child is blocking one, the dog has an alternative route.

- Make sure there's a safe place, like a playpen or crib, for the parent to leave the baby when she steps out of the room. Even then, however, the parent should still take the dog with her.

Remind parents that management is not perfect. In fact, one of our sayings is that "management almost always fails." Sooner or later, someone will only partially close a door, neglect to reposition the baby gate, forget to attach a leash, or otherwise veer from the plan. It happens all the time.

For this reason, we recommend using two (or more) forms of management for dogs who have behavioral concerns. For example, when a friend of mine has a babysitter, she puts her dog in the master bathroom with a Kong, closes the bathroom door, closes the bedroom door, and also puts a baby gate in front of it. This is not because the dog is trying to escape the bathroom, but rather because in the past a sitter inadvertently forgot about the dog and entered the bedroom. If my friend had merely left the dog in the bedroom, the dog would have gotten loose when the sitter opened the door. Accidents happen; it's important to have a secondary measure of control in place.

Management is a moving target: the things you need to do with a 9-day-old infant are different from what you do for a 9-month-old or a 9-year-old. Encourage parents to think ahead.

Children develop in fairly predictable patterns. It's common for a baby to roll over before crawling, to walk before running, and to ride a tricycle before rollerblading. These behaviors are normal, yet imagine the family dog's surprise as these changes occur. There's no way to give the dog prior

Baby gates are helpful tools

warning. Instead, parents need to anticipate the next stage of the child's development and start making changes beforehand. For example, baby gates should appear before the baby learns to crawl. The dog should be taught not to dart out the door before the child is actually tall enough to open that door.

The Sixth Thing Dogs Wish People Knew is . . .
Teens Can Be as Tough as Toddlers
● ● ● ● ● ● ● ● ● ● ● ● ● ● ● ● ● ● ● ●

Many dog aficionados have the mistaken belief that if we just teach kids what to do with their dogs, they'll do it. That sounds good in theory, but the reality is more complex. Parents can get very discouraged when they're trying to set everyone up for success because it is hard work. Minute after minute, hour after hour, day after day, and year after year, it can be exhausting at times. Kids may mean well, but they're impulsive, immature, and inconsistent—after all, they're children!

Parents should not get a dog unless they themselves are committed to having a dog. Adults have the ultimate responsibility for any pet

in a household. "A dog for the kids" only works if the parents are really behind that dog.

I get very sad when I hear a parent threaten a child with the loss of the family dog. I am a firm believer in consequences, but let's make sure the punishment fits the crime. I think it's fair to say that you can't have dinner until the dogs are fed, you won't watch TV for the weekend because you didn't scoop the yard (after being reminded twice), or you have

A "dog for the kids" requires a family commitment

to vacuum the living room because you were grumpy about letting the dogs out for a potty break. These are time-limited consequences that don't change the basic structure of the household. Are you really going to rehome a dog because a child is forgetful or inconsistent? What will you do when the child is forgetful about homework or inconsistent about manners?

Dog aficionados understand this. I don't like the title, but Karen Pryor's *Don't Shoot the Dog* has a really good point. Shooting the dog—or in this case, rehoming the dog—solves the parent's short-term problem, but in a really drastic, permanent way that will likely harm the relationship between parent and child. It's not a dog aficionado's job to be the family counselor, but far too often, we find ourselves in that role.

Dog aficionados spend a lot of time looking at how to set dogs up for success. A large part of that is setting clear expectations and then giving lots of feedback. There's always a significant difference in the amount of feedback an owner and I give a dog while training. I have to beg and plead with the owner to reward the dog at even half or a third of the rate I use. Once they increase their rate of reinforcement, the dog begins to learn faster.

Carabiner Tip #1

Use a carabiner clip to create a cheap and easy waist leash. As long as you don't have any back problems, walking a dog using a waist leash can be a great idea. It's nice to have your hands free for opening doors, pushing a stroller, or scooping poop.

Teaching children is the same. Telling them once what they need to do is not enough. Let's encourage parents to coach kids on proper interactions with dogs (just as we are coaching the parents to become better dog trainers). A coach gives a steady stream of feedback, both positive and negative, and tweaks behavior over time. Dogs, children, and even adults will need lots of practice to learn

DoggoneSafe.com's Supervision Guidelines

Many parents wonder when a child is old enough to interact with or walk a dog without supervision. Unfortunately there is no "one size fits all" rule. You are going to have to evaluate both your child and your dog to decide when the time is right.

DoggoneSafe.com suggests

- When the child can read the dog's body language
- When the child and dog have a mutually respectful relationship
- When the dog will happily and willingly follow directions from the child
- If the dog has never shown any sign of aggression toward people or other dogs and does not chase cars, cats, or other animals
- When the child knows how to interpret situations and take appropriate action.

Most kids under 12 will not meet these criteria.

new skills, and feedback is an important part of developing better habits.

As dog aficionados, we need to remind parents that the relationship between their kids and dogs will continually evolve and that they'll be offering guidance right up until their child moves out of the house. Unfortunately, there is no age during childhood at which you can say, "Phew, I'm done with the kid-and-dog stuff." There will always be things a parent should be watching. For example, with my 17-year-old, I have to keep an eye on his body language because at times he can unintentionally frighten a dog by looming. When it happens (or looks likely to happen), I make sure he notices so he can change his behavior to be less intimidating.

The other thing parents need to know is that monitoring interactions between kids and dogs gets harder as the child grows up.

We spend so much time talking about infants and dogs that we don't address the fact that older kids are the ones populating the dog-bite statistics.

The older kids are, the more complex kid-and-dog relationships become. We need our clients to know that. If we do not, they can be left feeling that there's something wrong with their family. To them, it seems so easy for everyone else, yet in their household, they are still actively managing and intervening. Let them know it's normal and necessary to make changes over time.

A friend of mine has a German shepherd who can be a little fear-aggressive with unfamiliar people. When her kids were younger, managing the dog was relatively easy because their friends would call to arrange play dates. She always knew when kids were coming over and could plan accordingly. She

Carabiner Tip #2

I love front-clip harnesses, but they can be difficult to properly fit. Using a carabiner to connect the harness to the dog's collar gives your clients a little extra peace of mind knowing that, on the off chance the harness slips, the leash will be connected to the dog's collar through the carabiner.

Practice fitting harnesses! Your clients will appreciate your help getting a secure, comfortable fit for their dog.

Kids & Dogs: A Professional's Guide to Helping Families

The People-Food Problem

When I encourage clients to be creative with what they use as treats or in food-dispensing toys, they often say they don't want their dog to have any "people food." This is another area where dog aficionados and dog owners may not see eye to eye.

I'm boggled by the idea that my dogs can tell—by taste apparently—the intended recipient of a food source. Somehow owners believe dogs are able to distinguish between products manufactured for people and for dogs. Because of this, many dog owners are leery of allowing their dog to eat any people food for fear that the dogs will turn up their noses at dog products from that point on.

Many products manufactured for dogs are filled with chemicals and preservatives. Not to mention the fact the price per pound of dog treats can be higher than the price of prime rib! Dogs could benefit from having more (healthy) people food and fewer processed dog treats, but the idea seems to violate the rules as most owners know them.

For years dog aficionados have told people not to feed their dogs "from the table." There's a huge difference between giving food off of your plate to a begging dog versus using tiny bits of a cheese stick as a reward or putting peanut butter in a Kong! Encourage your clients to pay more attention to how the dog gets a reward than who the food was originally prepared for.

was able to put both of her dogs in another room before the guests arrived.

Now that her kids are older, when the doorbell rings, there's often a child standing right there. Not a good situation for a fearful shepherd. Consequently, my friend's children have to take a more active role in managing the dogs *before* opening the front door. The responsibility has moved from the adult to the kids to ensure that the dogs' needs are met. Because of that, managing the dogs at the door is a lot tougher than it used to be.

Parents have to be actively involved in the relationship between their kids and dog forever. The needs evolve as the kids grow, but they never go away. And in many ways, the tasks get harder as the kids develop more autonomy.

It's normal, it's natural, but I don't think parents know to expect that. Let's tell them.

If Not You, Then Who?

● ● ● ● ● ● ● ● ● ● ● ● ● ● ● ● ● ● ●

Have I overwhelmed you? I hope not! I know you already have enough to do without me asking you to do even more. I am not trying to make anyone feel pressured, and yet I always come back to the question of who will help the dogs if we do not?

I have had dog aficionados tell me that teaching these six things to parents isn't their responsibility, that instead it is "the family's responsibility to make it work." While I agree that the ultimate responsibility does fall on the family, shelters are full of dogs whose families did not know how to fulfill that responsibility. In many cases, if a dog aficionado had stepped in with a little advice at the right moment, the end result would have been different. Each of us can have profound effects on dogs' lives, just by doing the work we feel passionate about.

Must Love Kids?

Dog aficionados sometimes tell me that they are not patient enough to work with children. That amuses me because most of what I do with kids stems from the fact that I tend toward impatience myself. Mother Teresa, I am not.

When I'm working with clients, I want the kids to be involved—after all, the dog is living with these children, so I want to see the relationship as it really is—but I also don't want to have kids running rampant and being distracting. If I leave the kids to their own devices, it's likely that I won't be happy with the results. So my solution is to keep the kids busy doing things I'd like them to do. I give specific instructions to each child, rotate activities every few minutes, and keep things as light-hearted as possible.

I love working with kids—I really do—but it was an acquired skill. Give it a try. I hope you'll come to enjoy it too.

Beginning with breeders, shelter personnel, and rescue workers, we can work to make sure that dogs are matched with the right families. I see questionable matches all the time, like the adolescent boxer mix who was paired with the legally blind senior citizen who lives alone in a condo. How will she adequately exercise him?

Or the 9-month-old German shepherd with mouthing issues who was placed with 1- and 3-year-old children. Or the family with four kids under 8 who wanted to adopt a pair of Jack Russell terrier littermates. Placements such as these aren't good for the people or for the dog.

When you step in, ask questions, and share your knowledge, often you can help families make choices that better meet their needs, which increases the odds that their dog will have a long, happy life in that household. Tell potential adopters to look for dogs who *adore* children, not just tolerate them on the first introduction, in order to increase the likelihood the dog will be able to put up with the things that even the best kids inevitably do.

The standards are higher for a dog that lives with kids. Not every dog can do

Keeping Kids Busy

I strongly encourage dog trainers to welcome children in their lessons. Get them actively involved! Here are a few ideas:

- Give a child a timer and ask her to count how many sits the dog can do in 10 seconds
- Take turns! Just as dogs lose focus easily, so do children. Switch activities often.
- Use kids as distractions. Ask a child to walk, run, hop, hula-hoop, or spin while you are teaching the dog to focus 5-10' away.
- Ask a child to be the official record keeper by writing down how many times the dog does each behavior in a lesson; what the dog's three favorite treat, toy, and activities are; things to practice for homework; and anything else you can think of.

Kids are distracting. No doubt about it. But keep in mind that the dog is living with these kids. We can either teach them how to behave around dogs or cross our fingers and hope for the best. I know which the dogs would vote for.

Kids & Dogs: A Professional's Guide to Helping Families

Share the Load

Far too many dog aficionados become frustrated and burn out. This is a terrible loss for all of us—and I think it's largely avoidable if we make an effort to reach out and support one another.

For 8 years, I worked alone. While I loved my clients and their dogs, at times it was a very lonely job. I often doubted my abilities because I didn't have anyone to bounce ideas off of.

I'm really shy, so I had to force myself to contact other trainers and invite them out for lunch. To my delight, I found that they were as eager to talk about dogs as I was.

As a result, I now have a wonderful group of supportive "dog-friends." Together we laugh and cry about our experiences working with dogs and their families. Being with them fills me up and make me strong enough to face the challenges ahead. I strongly encourage you to find people who will give you the energy, ideas, and motivation you need to keep doing the important work you do.

it. Not every dog *wants* to do it. We need to match the dogs who will thrive in a family environment with families looking for dogs.

And then we need to go the extra mile to make sure those dogs are well understood and cared for by the families who love them, but don't always know how to set their dogs up for success.

We need to be on the lookout for little ways we can help each dog we meet. In my opinion, the most valuable thing we can do is teach everyone a little bit about dog body language. I believe teaching owners to read their dogs is far more important that teaching sit, down, stay, and come. My clients come in asking for basic obedience. They'll get that, but they'll also get a general understanding of body language. I give them what they want *and* what they need.

The things I'm asking you to do are, in my opinion, the most important things we can do as dog aficionados:

➤ Let people know that dogs are communicating all the time. Their language is not hard to learn, but it's not necessarily intuitive either.

- Remember that parents have very good intentions, but they need your help. Everybody makes mistakes: not because they don't care, but because they don't know what they should do.
- Be supportive and open. Once people know you are there as a resource and not as a judge, they will turn to you for support.
- Help dogs by serving as interpreters between them and the people who love, but don't always understand, them.

True bliss: It doesn't happen automatically, but families can get there with your help

Appendix A
Good Moment/Bad Moment

● ● ● ● ● ● ● ● ● ● ● ● ● ● ● ● ● ● ● ●

Photos and videoclips are terrific tools for teaching people about canine body language. By capturing a moment in time, they offer you the opportunity to ask, "Is the dog enjoying this interaction, tolerating it, or saying, 'enough already'?"

You'll be working against some common, deeply held myths about dog behavior:

➤ Behaviors that are intended kindly will always be welcome
➤ Dogs enjoy the same interactions with familiar people and strangers
➤ Good dogs are happy and comfortable in all situations

People always interpret behavior through their own experiences and emotions. It's inevitable. Unfortunately an emotional connection often skews how people interpret what they see.

Few people believe that their dog doesn't enjoy a great big hug. Yet they can clearly see when another dog is uncomfortable in a similar situation. Why? Because to believe that their dog doesn't like *hugs* could imply that their dog doesn't like *them*! This is like comparing apples and oranges, but you'll encounter this problem often.

Tread carefully here! People love their dogs. If they feel like

> ## Cheat Sheets for Dog Aficionados
>
> These two handy, laminated pocket guides will be invaluable for helping your clients understand dog body language.
>
> • **Family Dog Cheat Sheet**
> • **Off-Leash Dog Play**
>
> Check them out at www.dreamdogproductions.com

you are telling them their dog doesn't like them, they'll stop listening. I know that's not what you are saying, but that may be what they hear.

Use photos, videos, and even other people's dogs to educate your clients about body language. Encourage people to evaluate whether they are seeing a good moment or a bad moment and remind them that we all have bad moments.

In the end, the most important thing to remember is that all good dogs have bad moments, and good owners help their dogs through those moments to the best of their ability.

Kids & Dogs: A Professional's Guide to Helping Families

Good Moment

Bad Moment

Good Moment

Bad Moment

Good Moment

Bad Moment

Good Moment

Bad Moment

Kids & Dogs: A Professional's Guide to Helping Families

Good Moment

Bad Moment

Good Moment

Bad Moment

Kids & Dogs: A Professional's Guide to Helping Families

Good Moment

Bad Moment

Good Moment

Bad Moment

Kids & Dogs: A Professional's Guide to Helping Families

Good Moment

Bad Moment

Good Moment

Bad Moment

Kids & Dogs: A Professional's Guide to Helping Families

Appendix B
Going to School

● ● ● ● ● ● ● ● ● ● ● ● ● ● ● ● ● ●

I encourage dog aficionados to go to schools and libraries to teach kids about dogs. Kids love to learn about dogs. Imagine all the kids we could reach if each of us did just two visits per year!

There's a lot of debate among trainers about whether to bring a dog on these visits. There are some very good arguments on each side of the issue. Any visit will entail a certain amount of excitement and stress for the dog (and probably for you as well). It's really important to know whether the event will be too stressful for your dog, and if so, don't bring a dog! Whenever I take a dog anywhere, my primary responsibility is to make sure the dog feels safe, comfortable, and happy.

It's important to teach kids to be safe around dogs

But I also know there's a real value to offering children the opportunity to practice meeting an unfamiliar dog under very controlled circumstances with a knowledgeable person orchestrating the interaction. If kids don't get a chance to interact with a dog under a dog aficionado's supervision, then their first chance to try the three steps for meeting a new dog will be with an unprepared neighbor, who may not know how to set everyone up for success or recognize when things aren't going well.

> ## Be a Tree
>
> If you aren't sure what you'd say when faced with a roomful of kids, check out Doggone Safe's Be A Tree program. It's a complete kit with everything you'll need to do a presentation for kids without bringing a live dog. The kit includes many large, clear photos of dogs and a complete script so you'll always know what to say next. Go to www.doggonesafe.com to learn more about it.

I am lucky enough to have highly social dogs, so, for me, I think the benefits of bringing a dog outweigh the challenges.

PRESCHOOL AND KINDERGARTEN SCRIPT

This is a basic outline of what I say when speaking to a group of young children (from 3 to 6 years old). My sessions for older kids are very similar, but I vary the content more based on their questions.

When visiting a preschool or kindergarten class, I typically bring a stuffed dog in addition to one of my own dogs. I want the kids to have two chances to practice petting a dog in a safe, controlled environment.

I bring a long rope to separate the dog's area from the kids'. I am very clear that kids cannot cross the rope until they are invited to do so at the end of the presentation. With a preschool or kindergarten class, the kids and I typically sit on the floor. With older kids, I usually stand and they sit in chairs.

I typically spend 20-25 minutes with each class. Longer is not better. Keep things moving quickly to maintain the kids' interest.

Each of my dogs has done many school visits, but because Gordo has more years of experience, he gets the privilege of having his name used throughout the script. (Poor Edzo!)

Me: First I want to talk about strangers. Are you allowed to talk to strangers?

Kids: *Usually the kids will all say no. Sometimes one will say, "If my mom is with me."*

Me: What if you were playing in your front yard and a stranger came up to talk to you? Who should you tell?

I have learned to ask, "who should you tell" rather than "what should you do?" Otherwise I would occasionally get answers like, "I'd kick him and run away."

Kids: *My mom, my parents, my grandma.*

Me: That's right. You always want to tell a trusted adult, like your parents, or your teacher, or a neighbor.

Use a rope to separate the kid zone from the dog zone on school visits

I always add the teacher to the list.

Me: What if the stranger was a dog? What if you were playing in your front yard and a strange dog ran up to you? Are you allowed to play with that dog?

Kids: *Huge variety of responses.*

Me: Right, you cannot play with a dog unless it is with an adult and your parents say it is okay.

Now here's a tricky question: What if it's a dog you know? What if it's Cocoa, and she lives next door, and you play with her all the time? Could you play with her if she was out without an adult and your parents weren't there?

Kids: *They almost know that they cannot pet the dog in this case.*

Me: Even if it's a dog you know, you have to treat it like a stranger if you don't have an adult with you. So first you have to tell the dog that you can't play and then you have to go tell an adult that the dog is loose.

But how would you tell the dog that you can't play with it? Do dogs use words?

Kids: *Most of the kids laugh and say no. Often one child will say they bark as a form of talking.*

Me: Would a dog understand if I said, "Go away. I can't play with you because you aren't with a grownup? Go home." Would a dog understand my words?

I turn and talk to my dog at this point. The dog usually ignores me.

Me: Dogs use their bodies to communicate with each other. We use our bodies to communicate too. I'm going to act out a few emotions, and I want you to tell me how I feel.

Then I pantomime three or four emotions: happiness, by spreading my hands apart and putting a huge smile on my face; fear, by moving back, turning away from the kids, and glancing repeatedly at them; anger, by furrowing my brow, glaring, and shaking my finger at them; and sadness, by frowning, slumping my shoulders, and gazing downward. The kids are excellent at identifying the emotions.

Me: Dogs are really good at using their bodies to communicate and reading our bodies for clues too. So if I want a dog to go away, I need to use my body to tell the dog that I can't play with it.

With older kids, I ask what I should do if I wanted to get a dog very excited. We talk about how to rev a dog up. Then I ask them how well they think a dog would distinguish between excitement-inducing behaviors and a person who ran away screaming. They can easily see that running is NOT the desired way to tell a dog to go away. I don't talk with young children about a dog chasing them.

Me: I'm going to teach you how to use your body to tell a dog that it needs to go away now. Everybody stand up. We're going to be a tree. First you plant your feet.

I stomp my feet, first left, then right, with young kids because I want them to practice getting their feet firmly placed. I don't think kids actually need to stomp to get into the "be a tree" pose, but I want it to be distinctly different from just standing there.

The "Be a Tree" pose—feet planted, arms clasped in front of the body, and eyes looking down toward the ground

When you are working with young kids, take along a stuffed dog for extra practice

Me: Fold your arms in front of your body. Now look down at the ground. Can you see my dog while you are looking down at the ground? I bet some of you can.

When you can see the dog while you are looking down, then you have to stay still and be a tree until you can't see the dog anymore. When you can't see the dog, then you can *walk* away and tell an adult. If the dog comes back, then you have to be a tree again until the dog goes away.

Okay, now we're going to practice. Look, I see a loose dog!

I move the stuffed dog around and bring it over to "sniff" a few kids. One of them often giggles and moves away. I remind them to stand still and be a tree so that the dog will go away.

Me: What should we do? Be a tree. Plant your feet. Wrap your arms around you. Look down at the ground. That's great! Look, you all know how to be a tree. Let's do it one more time.

We all practice being a tree again, and I say each step every time I do it with the kids so that it'll stick in their brains!

Me: Okay, let's all sit back down. Now you know what to do if you see a loose dog: you have to be a tree, wait for the dog to go away, and then tell an adult. Sometimes the dog will wait a while to see if you are going to change your mind.

Again I demonstrate solicitous, wiggly behavior with stuffed dog.

Me: Just wait. Stay still and be a good tree. The dog will go away and then you can go tell an adult.

There are lots of times you can be a tree. Have you ever gone to a friend's house and had their dog jump on you when you came in the door? You could be a tree then. If you stand very still and be a tree, the parents will help calm the dog down.

Or have you ever gotten really silly at your house and had your dog get silly too? That happens at my house sometimes. If you ever want to tell your dog to stop being so silly, you can be a tree. Your dog will understand that your body is saying it is time to settle down.

Most of the dogs you see, though, aren't loose, are they? Most of the time you see dogs on leashes walking with their owners. What if you want to pet one of those dogs? What should you do?

Kids: *Miscellaneous answers.*

Me: First you have to ask the owner, "May I pet your dog?" Sometimes the answer will be no! That's okay. Some dogs don't live with kids and don't know how to act with them. Some dogs think kids are scary! Are you scary?

Kids: *No, no, no!*

This part makes the kids laugh. They can't imagine that a dog could find them scary.

Me: But some dogs don't know that, and they might be a little worried. So if their owner says no, that's okay. There are lots of other dogs who like to be petted by kids.

It's important for you to know that if an owner says no, they aren't saying that you aren't a good friend for dogs. They are only saying their dog gets worried about meeting new people.

If the owner says yes, then you have to ask the dog. But we just said that dogs don't understand our words. How could we ask a dog with our body if it's okay to pet it? We need to use body language. Put your hand out in front of you in a fist with your fingers pointed down. See if the dog wants to come sniff your hand.

Then I demonstrate with the stuffed dog, coming forward, being waggy, etc.

Me: Did this dog say yes or no?

Kids: *Yes.*

Me: What if the dog backed up and hid behind its owner? Is that dog saying yes or no?

Kids: *No.*

Me: What if the dog barked at you?

Then I actually bark, using a high-pitched staccato bark. My dog is used to my antics and ignores me.

Kids: *No.*

Me: Right. We never pet a barking dog—even your own dog. Never, ever pet a barking dog!

So if the person said yes and the dog said yes, now you can pet the dog. You can just turn your hand over and try stroking alongside the dog's neck, or rubbing under its chin or on its chest. You can also pet a dog on its back.

What about tails? Can we pet dogs on their tail?

Kids: *No.*

Me: Right. We don't pet dogs on their tails. We also have to be really careful of a dog's sensitive eyes and ears. Most dogs don't like to be petted on top of their heads, and lots of people do it.

I demonstrate with stuffed dog thunk-thunk-thunk on head.

Me: I'll show you with my dog. Gordo is my friend. I love him and I never hurt him or scare him, but watch his face if I pat him on his head.

I demonstrate with my real dog. Gordo will close his mouth and blink his eyes. He'll be extremely **tolerant**, *but it will be clear, even to young children, that he is not* **enjoying** *the interaction.*

Me: How happy was he? Did Gordo like for me to pet him on top of his head?

Kids: *He didn't like it.*

Me: Now we're going to practice petting dogs. Your teacher is going

Avoid reaching toward a dog's sensitive eyes and ears when petting

to have my stuffed dog, and I'll be here with Gordo. First you'll go over to your teacher and say, "May I pet your dog?" What do you think she will say?

Kids: Yes!

Me: Then you'll put your hand out for the pretend dog to sniff. Then you can pet the pretend dog.

Little kids always have to pet the stuffed dog before petting my dog. With kids over 6, I don't make them pet the stuffed dog. I ask the teacher to give me a heads up if any kid is rough or pets on top of the head, so I can set them up for success with the real dog. Most do very well.

Me: After you've petted the pretend dog, you can come over to me. I will say, "Would you like to pet my dog?" I hope you'll say yes.

I always turn it around so that I ask the child rather than expect them to ask me. It's stressful for many children to talk with strangers, so some kids who would dearly love to pet the dog will be too frightened to talk to me. It's much easier to for them to be able to simply nod in response to my question.

Me: Then you'll put your fist out to let Gordo sniff it. He'll probably say yes, and then you can pet Gordo.

Many trainers prefer that kids do not extend a hand toward a dog and would rather have the child stand still with hands at the sides and allow the dog to approach the child. This is far too similar to the "be a tree" pose for me.

We need to teach kids what they need to do to tell a dog to go away as well as something different that they should do when they would like to interact with a dog. I encourage them to stop at a distance to ask the owner and then extend their fist without stepping toward the dog. If the dog is interested, I allow him to approach the child.

With older kids, I ask, "Do you think the dog can smell faster if I move faster? Would it help if I go like this?" Then I demonstrate a punching motion. The kids think that is ridiculously funny. Then we talk about how it's important to avoid abrupt or startling movements around dogs.

In the rare case when my dog says no, it's usually because he got distracted. I simply ask the child to step back and try it again.

Me: I'd like to only have one or two kids petting Gordo at a time. After you've had your turn, then you'll need to go back and sit down so that all of the kids can have a turn.

The class takes turns going first to their teacher and then to me for a turn to pet the dog. For a frightened child, I tell them that their teacher could fold her hand over his or hers so that Gordo will sniff both hands (and a cold nose won't touch the child's hand).

I will also offer to turn Gordo away and let the frightened child pet his back and hips. This is not how I want kids to meet dogs, but when a child is interested, but nervous, it can be beneficial for him or her to have the chance to actually pet a dog and find out that it's not so scary. I only do that for children who seem to want to pet the dog, but are too uncomfortable to approach.

I am very clear that no child will be required or coerced to pet a dog. When one is afraid, be sure that a well-meaning teacher isn't pressuring the child to interact with the dog.

Me: Okay, now, before I go, I want to see one more time what you do if you see a loose dog.

Everyone gets up to be a tree. I thank them for letting Gordo and me visit their class. Then we leave.

Visual Learner?

Visit www.dreamdogproductions.com
for a DVD that contains an interview about
doing school events and footage of one of
my preschool visits.

Kids & Dogs: A Professional's Guide to Helping Families

Appendix C
Resources

● ● ● ● ● ● ● ● ● ● ● ● ● ● ● ● ●

Books, Magazines, & Pocket Guides

Animal Sheltering, www.animalsheltering.org

Bond with Your Dog, Victoria Schade, www.lifeontheleash.com

Family Dog Cheat Sheet, Colleen Pelar,
  www.dreamdogproductions.com

For the Love of a Dog, Patricia McConnell,
  www.patriciamcconnell.com

Great Dog Adoptions, Sue Sternberg, www.suesternberg.com

Living with Kids and Dogs . . . Without Losing Your Mind, Colleen
  Pelar, www.livingwithkidsanddogs.com

Off-Leash Dog Play, Robin Bennett and Susan Briggs,
  www.dreamdogproductions.com

Off-Leash Dog Play Pocket Guide, Robin Bennett and Susan
  Briggs, www.dreamdogproductions.com

Play with Your Dog, Pat Miller,
  www.peaceablepaws.com

Whole Dog Journal,
  www.wholedogjournal.com

Training Academies

All Dogs Academy,
  www.alldogsacademy.com

Peaceable Paws Academy, www.peaceablepaws.com

San Francisco Training Academy, www.sfspca.org/academy

WEBSITES

Doggone Safe, www.doggonesafe.com

Dogs and Storks, www.dogsandstorks.com

Dream Dog Productions, www.dreamdogproductions.com

Living with Kids and Dogs, www.livingwithkidsanddogs.com

Pawlicker Dog Toys, www.pawlickers.com

Premier Pet Products, www.premier.com

Index

yawn, 68, 72, 76

Colleen Pelar, CPDT, CDBC

● ● ● ● ● ● ● ● ● ● ● ● ● ● ● ● ● ● ●

With more than 18 years of experience helping parents navigate the challenges living with kids and dogs, Colleen Pelar has honed a unique perspective filled with humor and practical, easy-to-implement tips for success. Colleen wants to ensure that kids and dogs have happy, healthy relationships.

A lifelong dog lover, Colleen spent more than a decade alternately frustrated by the scarcity of guidance offered to parents and disappointed by the unrealistic—and sometimes dangerous—advice given in the very few books that addressed kids and dogs. Colleen found this lack of support unacceptable and so she began gathering data to write her book, *Living with Kids and Dogs...Without Losing Your Mind*.

Living with Kids and Dogs is the only book that covers the dog-related needs of each stage of childhood from birth through the teen years. Recognizing that this book filled a pressing need, the Humane Society of the United States bestowed its prestigious Compassionate Care Award on Colleen. *Living with Kids and Dogs*

is also a proud winner of the 2006 Parent-to-Parent Adding Wisdom Award, the only award program ever honored by Disney. com.

As co-owner of All About Dogs, LLC, the largest dog-training facility in northern Virginia, Colleen oversees numerous group classes, private lessons, behavioral evaluations, and behavior modification programs. Named one of the best training facilities in the D.C. area by Washingtonian magazine, All About Dogs caters to families and looks for ways to help parents successfully integrate a dog into their busy lives.

Colleen gives presentations around the country, educating people about how to live safely with kids and dogs. She is also an instructor at the Washington D.C. Metropolitan Police Academy where she teaches police officers how to interact with the many dogs they'll encounter on the job.

An active member of the Association of Pet Dog Trainers (APDT) and the International Association of Animal Behavior Consultants (IAABC), Colleen regularly attends dog-training seminars and has earned the Certified Pet Dog Trainer (CPDT) and Certified Dog Behavior Consultant (CDBC) titles.

She lives a semi-chaotic life with her husband, Jack; their sons, Justin, Kyle, and Brandon; and, of course, their dogs, Gordo and Edzo.

Contact Colleen

Dream Dog Productions
PO Box 4227
Woodbridge VA 22194
703-980-0908
www.dreamdogproductions.com

DREAMDOG
PRODUCTIONS